The Ministry of Jesus

A Devotional Study

CHARLES FRANCIS WHISTON

*Associate Professor of Moral Theology,
Church Divinity School of the Pacific,
Berkeley, California*

THE PILGRIM PRESS · BOSTON

247.235
W579

117252

Printed in the United States of America

This book is dedicated to
Jesus
as a thank offering for the
life, friendship, and ministry of
Henry Herbert Shires
long time Dean of the
Church Divinity School of the Pacific,
and now Suffragan Bishop of the
Diocese of California

CONTENTS

A Book of Devotion   C. F. W.   ix

Prologue   xiii

PART ONE   THE BEGINNINGS

1   The Baptism of Jesus 1
2   The Temptations 4

PART TWO   THE GALILEAN MINISTRY

3   God's First Word — Repentance 11
4   Jesus Calls Four Disciples 11
5   Casting out an Unclean Spirit 14
6   Healings in Capernaum 15
7   Jesus at Prayer 17
8   Healing a Leper 18
9   A Paralytic and Forgiveness 20
10   The Calling of Matthew and the Criticism That
     Followed 25
11   Teaching Concerning Fasting 26
12   Patches and Wine 28
13   Sabbath-Day Laws 29
14   Healing on the Sabbath 30
15   Withdrawal from the Synagogues 32
16   Choosing Twelve Disciples 33
17   Beelzebul 34
18   Family Opposition 36
19   The Parable of the Sower 38
20   The Kingdom of God 40

21	Mustard Seed	41
22	A Storm at Sea	42
23	Nazareth	43
24	The Death of John the Baptist	44

Part Three WITHDRAWAL FROM GALILEE

25	A Summary of the Period	47
26	Seeking Retreat Across the Lake	48
27	Impossibility of Escape	49
28	A Sacred Meal	50
29	Jesus on the Beach	53
30	The First Preaching of the Cross	54
31	The Pharisees Seek after a Sign	55
32	Woe to Three Galilean Towns	56
33	Commandments of God and Traditions of Men	56
34	Transfiguration	58
35	Healing	62

Part Four PERIOD OF WANDERING

36	The Syrophenician Woman	65
37	Healing a Dumb Man	66
38	Caesarea Philippi	67
39	Satanic Temptation	69
40	Prophecy of Death and Resurrection	71

Part Five JOURNEY TO JERUSALEM

41	Greatness	73
42	Divorce	74
43	Little Children	77
44	A Rich Young Ruler	78

45 Entrance into the Kingdom 80
46 Rewards 81
47 Death Ahead 82
48 Self-Seeking 84
49 Jealousy 85
50 Now or Never 86
51 Zacchaeus 87
52 Bartimaeus 90

PART SIX   JERUSALEM

53 Entrance into Jerusalem 93
54 Cleansing the Temple 95
55 Authority 97
56 Parable of the Vineyard 98
57 God and Caesar 100
58 A Woman Taken in Adultery 101
59 An Academic Question 104
60 The Great Commandment 106
61 Davidic Descent 107
62 Giving 108
63 The Temple 109
64 The Parable of the Fig Tree 110
65 Strategy 111
66 Bethany 112
67 Judas Iscariot 114
68 Preparing the Passover 116
69 Foot-Washing 117
70 Prophecy of Betrayal 119
71 Bread — Body; Wine — Blood 120

72 Prophecy to Peter 122
73 Gethsemane 124
74 Betrayal Consummated 127
75 Denial by Peter 129
76 Condemnation by the Council 130
77 Brought to Pilate 132
78 Mocking 134
79 Crucifixion 135
80 Death 137
81 Burial 140

Part Seven God's Mighty Act

82 The Women at the Tomb 143
83 Resurrection 144
84 The First Appearance 147
85 Forgiveness 150
86 The Ascension 151

Epilogue   153

A BOOK OF DEVOTION

THE MINISTRY OF JESUS is offered to the reader as a book of *devotion*, and it is hoped that it will be read in the mood and temper of devotion. It is intended to serve as a companion book to TEACH US TO PRAY. Those who have read that book will remember the stress it laid upon feeding the life of prayer regularly and persistently upon the gospel records of the life and work of Jesus. It is Jesus, and no other, who clearly and sharply focuses for us our knowledge of God. Our prayers are addressed to God *through* Jesus. The term " through Jesus Christ " means something far deeper and more significant than a formula of prayer. Rather it implies that we shall by study and devotion sit often at the feet of Jesus, as he has been revealed to us through the gospel records, and saturate our whole life of praying with the spirit and the truth that is in him. Unless our faith in the risen, ascended, reigning, interceding Christ is anchored firmly in the ministry of the historic Jesus, our imagination will often lead us astray into unprofitable speculation. The Church of Jesus the Christ has humbly and graciously placed in our hands the four gospel records, and bids us go with meekness and docility to the school of Jesus.

Our four gospel records are ostensibly collections of memoirs of early Christians of the first century. In no way do they claim to be scientific history. Rather they are unashamedly written from the perspective of loving faith in the person Jesus, the Christ of God. Often the events described in them are arranged topically instead of chronologically. Presented as they customarily are in our English Bibles, in chapters and verses, the reader inevitably finds himself assuming that the events follow each other in close chronological sequence. Rather we need to read them as a collection of incidents. In this book therefore each event is taken as a unit, and only when there is substantial historical and psychological evidence are they treated as having chronological sequence — notably in the later part of Jesus' ministry. It is believed that such a plan best serves to help and increase our devotional insight.

Despite the fact that many decades of serious critical study of the four Gospels have passed, yet little of the results of such study has filtered down to the level of the ordinary Christian layman. Instead men tend either to read the Gospels as scientific history, accepting all that they contain by faith; or, having a little knowledge by hearsay of the critical work that has been done, they tend to discount them entirely and cease to read the Gospels. We need seriously to wed critical study and devotional reading. Critical study is not an end in itself, but is intended to be the handmaid of devotion, so that by its aid men may come to know more truly the person and work of Jesus of Nazareth. THE MINISTRY OF JESUS is the product of over thirty years of this marriage of critical study and devotional reading. Because of that dual background it is believed that this book under God may serve to bless and enrich those many in our generation who " would see Jesus."

Because of the limitations of space, not all of the events recorded in the four Gospels have been treated, but enough have been selected to afford the reader a grasp of the principal lines of the work and teaching of Jesus, upon which the reader can then himself build the rest. In the main the events are chosen from the Gospel according to Mark, but where the tradition in the other records is believed to give a more truthful and deeper insight, the text of Mark has been abandoned. The translation used is that of the King James Version, but liberty has been taken of departing from the exact wording in the case of words which for us today carry a different meaning and would therefore lead us astray in interpreting a passage. In devotional reading it is believed that the matchless dignity and cadence of the King James Version render it best suited for a study such as is contemplated here.

Where biblical scholars today often disagree among themselves as to the interpretation of any event, and as to the evidence for that event, it cannot be expected that the interpretation of the passages selected will meet with whole-hearted approval. It is the belief of the author that good critical and devotional evidences lie behind the interpretations given. The purpose of the book is to lead readers to the feet of Jesus, so that they may confess Jesus to be their personal Lord and Saviour.

Over many years now two books have been of especial help in both study and devotional reading of the four Gospels. Those who are familiar with them will at once discern the heavy debt which this book owes to them. The first book is Charles Lewis Slattery's *The Master of the World;* the other is Walter Lowrie's *Jesus According to St. Mark.* Both books are now out of print. I wish to express my deep spiritual debt to both of these authors for that which they have taught me about Jesus. But most of all I would acknowledge the incalculable debt which I owe to Jesus, as over these thirty years I have sat at his feet to be taught of him.

CHARLES FRANCIS WHISTON

Berkeley, California

PROLOGUE

IN THE BEGINNING was the Word, and the Word was with God, and the Word was God. He was in the beginning with God; all things were made through him, and without him was not anything made that was made. In him was life, and the life was the light of men. The light shines in the darkness, and the darkness has not overcome it.

The true light that enlightens every man was coming into the world; he was in the world, and the world was made through him, yet the world knew him not; he came to his own home, and his own people received him not. But to all who received him, who believed in his name, he gave power to become children of God; who were born, not of blood nor of the will of the flesh nor of the will of man, but of God.

And the Word became flesh and dwelt among us, full of grace and truth; we have beheld his glory, glory as of the only Son from the Father.... And from his fullness have we all received, grace upon grace. For the law was given through Moses; grace and truth came through Jesus Christ. No one has ever seen God; the only Son, who is in the bosom of the Father, he has made him known.

John 1: 1-5, 9-14, 16-18[1]

---

[1] From *The Revised Standard Version of the New Testament*, copyright, 1946, by The International Council of Religious Education, and used by permission.

PART ONE

THE BEGINNINGS

1 THE BAPTISM OF JESUS

It came to pass in those days, that Jesus came from Nazareth of Galilee, and was baptized of John in Jordan. And straightway coming up out of the water, he saw the heavens opened, and the Spirit like a dove descending upon him: and there came a voice from heaven, saying, Thou art my beloved Son, in thee I am well pleased.

Mark 1: 9-11. Alt. by Luke 3: 22

Mark gives us only a very brief, terse account of this first recorded event of the ministry of Jesus. These few, short verses, however, tell us much. They record for us data of the utmost importance for a right understanding of all that will follow in his ministry.

At his baptism there was given to Jesus both the objective and the deep inner confirmation from God that he stood in a unique, incomparable relationship with God, such as is not shared by any other man. The uniqueness of this relationship which Jesus already has with God on the threshold of his ministry is obscured for us by our common translation of the Greek word *agapetos* into our English word "beloved." The Greek word carries a meaning and significance which our English translation does not. The Greek term implies that an object is beloved because there exists only *one* such object. Thus, if a person because of an accident had the use of only one eye, that eye would be his beloved eye. If parents had only one child, with no hope of having other children, that child would be the beloved child. We had best therefore translate the Greek word here by our English words "unique," "sole," or "only."

Neither in the New Testament nor in the Christian creeds is Jesus ever described as having only *our* kind of sonship with God, i.e., that by adoption and grace. It is the deep and unswerving conviction of Christian faith that Jesus is Son of God by nature, not by adoption. Jesus is not a mere man given by God honorary divinity.

Here in Mark is the first time that this distinctive word is used in the gospel record. It is a key word, used only very seldom and always in the Gospels used in this distinctive sense. We shall again meet with the word in the account of the Transfiguration, where it is used with God as the speaker, and for the purpose of correcting an erroneous conception about Jesus held by the three closest disciples. The only other usage in the Gospels occurs in the temple teaching of Jesus during the last week of his life upon earth, when he himself distinguishes his status from that of all previous servants and prophets of God by his statement, " Having yet therefore one son, his well-beloved, he sent him."

When and how Jesus first gained the knowledge of his in-comparable relationship with God, we do not know. Here we had best revere and follow the true agnosticism of the gospel writers. The New Testament is never an answer book to all the questions men can ask. Even the best human speculation cannot hope to give us certitude in these matters. There is nothing in the gospel records to compel us to infer that here for the first time, and as a surprise, Jesus gained this conviction. The one indubitable and indisputable fact which the Gospels record is that Jesus, upon beginning his ministry, already possesses the firm faith that he has a unique and incomparable relationship with God, that of beloved Son.

The deep and mysterious experiences of the inner life can only be interpreted and communicated to others by expressing and clothing them in terms of physical imagery. Jesus has clothed for us his baptismal experience in terms of a voice and of a vision. We are not, however, to presume to materialize in any crude fashion an experience which was essentially interior and spiritual. No microphone could have recorded that voice; no camera could have taken any picture.

"My beloved Son." Those words constitute the very central core of authority in the teaching that Jesus will bring to men from God. For what is it to be in the kingdom of God but to be in that fellowship in which God is absolutely sovereign, and man is lovingly and humbly obedient? That relationship Jesus already possesses. In Jesus, God's kingdom is come, although hidden from the eyes of men. Therefore he is enabled to proclaim with indisputable authority the true nature of life within that kingdom, and to call men to receive life within it from God through repentance. Jesus teaches that which he himself knows and knows authoritatively.

Although Jesus himself knows clearly and decisively his own unique relationship with God, yet *nobody else does.* We must empty our minds of the conception that they who first heard him and followed him knew from the beginning who Jesus truly was. Only very slowly, and only because of a revelation given by God, will the little band of chosen disciples learn who Jesus really is; and nothing short of God's mighty act of raising Jesus from death will give them the certainty that Jesus is the Christ of God.

Jesus grieved over men's sins; he felt the deep shame and dishonor that sin brought upon God, in a way that the hardened, sin-stained, deadened hearts of sinners had lost all power of doing. His first act as God's unique Son is that of making himself wholly one with the race of men. He owns the sins of men as his own sins and takes vicariously upon himself their full guilt; and he offers to God his perfect penitence for the sin of the whole world. He will not stand aloof and distant from sinful men; he presses his sinless life close to theirs, that their enslavement to sin may be broken.

2 THE TEMPTATIONS

Immediately the spirit driveth him into the wilderness.   Mark 1: 12

How may Jesus impart to men the holy fellowship which he himself has with God? He knew God; he also knew men. What shall be the principles and methods of his ministry to men? To determine that, Jesus withdraws from men and goes apart into the desolate hill country to be alone there with God.

Mark uses the vivid Greek verb *ekballo* to describe the inner pressure driving him into the wilderness. This withdrawal was not self-initiated, but rather was the strong pressure of God upon him. All throughout his ministry we shall find Jesus' life and work dominated by the will of God, and not grounded in human expediency or experiment. The life of Jesus is a completely theocentric life. In and through Jesus, God himself acts.

In those days he did eat nothing: and when they were ended, he afterward hungered. And the devil said unto him, If thou be the Son of God, command this stone that it be made bread. And Jesus answered him, saying, It is written, That man shall not live by bread alone, but by every word of God.

Luke 4: 2-4

Jesus fasted and prayed. So preoccupied was he with the will and purpose of God for his coming ministry that Jesus took no thought concerning his own physical needs. Fasting here, as also throughout his entire life, was no artificial, meritorious, religious practice. Rather his fasting resulted naturally and fittingly from his all-absorbing preoccupation with God. Out of such fasting there issued his discovery and acceptance of the principles that will characterize his whole ministry; and from them he will never for one instant swerve. They were gained through the ordeal of inner temptations, which he has described for us in three vivid, unforgettable pictures — stone and bread, a mountain-top experience, and standing on the pinnacle of the

Jerusalem temple. We must refrain from any attempt to materialize the three experiences. Though described for our sakes in fact-like imagery, they are essentially spiritual experiences.

All three temptations rise out of Jesus' peculiar instinct in knowing himself by faith to be the unique Son of God, and in having laid upon him the task of bringing to men the kingdom of God. What methods shall he use to accomplish this?

He knew well the dire poverty of his people, and of their life under the heavy political and economic enslavement of Rome. When men's basic, physical needs are unmet, can they be expected to give attention to things of the spirit? Bread is the symbol of all man's basic, physical needs; and these basic needs are so deep and important that Jesus later in his ministry, when teaching his disciples to pray, will instruct them unashamedly to ask their heavenly Father for bread.

Men will always follow those who promise the alleviation or fulfillment of their basic, physical needs. Jesus could have every assurance that if he gave men bread, he could have a mighty following of the masses of people in Galilee and Judea. Why not use the mighty powers, which were implied in his unique relationship with God, to turn stones into bread? The very stones about him on the Judean hillsides resembled in shape and size the oriental loaves of bread. For him therefore it was an apt imagery for temptation, though not for us today. If he truly were God's only Son, he had the power to do this. Why not exercise this power in some such way, to bribe men by bread to enter the kingdom of God?

Will even the fullest satisfaction of man's basic, physical needs ever bring men under the loving sovereignty of God? Would men with well-filled stomachs have also deep concern for the things of God? The first word, as also the last word, from God is not bread. God has another first word, and also many other words for men. The first word, we shall soon see, is *repentance*. Some of God's other words will be *forgiveness*, *faith, obedience, agape.*[1] Will men hear and obey these words from God simply by giving them bread?

History has again and again substantiated the truth of Jesus' keen, accurate insight in these matters. Many a public leader has attempted to build an earthly kingdom upon the allegiance of men, rooted in the giving of bread. History has seen every such kingdom fall and perish. Man's needs go so much further than those of the beasts. Man has not been made for bread. Man has been made for God, and only life with God in the fellowship of sons can ever set the heart of man at rest and give him peace.

And the devil, taking him up into an high mountain, shewed unto him all the kingdoms of the world in a moment of time. And the devil said unto him, All this power will I give thee, and the glory of them: for that is delivered unto me; and to whomsoever I will I give it. If thou therefore wilt worship me, all shall be thine. And Jesus answered and said unto him, Get thee behind me, Satan: for it is written, Thou shalt worship the Lord thy God, and him only shalt thou serve.

Luke 4: 5-8

Jesus has also described his temptations to us in the imagery of standing upon a mountain peak, and from that vantage point surveying the roads, valleys, and plains below, populous with people. He who controlled the arteries of commerce, the economic and political life of the towns and cities where men dwelt, would have power to coerce men and to dominate their lives. If he brought to these people the high, pure, demanding word from God, would they hear him or heed it? Would they repent? What if they would not repent? What then?

Why not compromise and accommodate the pure word of God? Instead of calling men to repent, which they would refuse to do, why not appeal to those motivations to which men will ever be ready and eager to respond — fear, avarice, rewards?

---

[1]*Agape* is the Greek word for God's love for man, translated in our English Bibles as " love " or " charity."

But, so doing, would they then have that kind of fellowship with God in the kingdom that he had come to give them? Would an allegiance rooted in self-interest and earthly rewards be able to receive the salvation that God sought to give them? No; God's first word was *repentance*. Until that word had been heard and obeyed, the kingdom of God his Father could not come. From the very beginning down to the very end of his ministry Jesus was utterly faithful to that first word from God.

———

And he brought him to Jerusalem, and set him on a pinnacle of the temple, and said unto him, If thou be the Son of God, cast thyself down from hence: for it is written, He shall give his angels charge over thee, to keep thee: and in their hands they shall bear thee up, lest at any time thou dash thy foot against a stone. And Jesus answering said unto him, It is said, Thou shalt not test the Lord thy God. And when the devil had ended all the temptation, he departed from him for a season.

Luke 4: 9-13

The third imagery of his temptations was that of standing in imagination upon the pinnacle of the Jerusalem temple, to use his unique power as Son of God to dazzle and amaze men by a miracle, so that they would follow him into the kingdom of God. If truly he were the Son of God, then there was scriptural warrant (Psalms 91: 10-11) for believing that God would not allow any injury to happen to him, even though he should jump from the pinnacle of the temple. Were not all the angels of God at his service to protect him, lest he dash his foot against a stone? At a later time in his ministry, in the agony of Gethsemane, did not Jesus have at his disposal legions of angels to protect him against his enemies? Then, as now, he would not invoke their help for his own personal safety.

None of the three forms of temptation reveal Jesus so truly human as this one does. Who of us is there who has not daydreamed, with himself as the miracle-performing hero, the center of all eyes? We lack only the power to actualize our daydreams. He, who had the power, rejected such daydreaming as a satanic temptation. Jesus knew that men could never be brought into holy fellowship with God through amazement and astonishment. This temptation is one that we shall find repeatedly recurring in his later ministry.

The Scriptures can be used by Satan to serve his purposes. Here Jesus sets us forever free from enslavement to all bare literalism of Scripture. He rejected the tempting thought from Satan, that because he stood in the unique status of only Son of God, therefore he was exempt from either suffering or death. Do we have here, on the very threshold of his ministry, the first sight from afar (as also the acceptance by anticipation) of the end of his ministry — the Cross? If he were utterly, unswervingly faithful to God, would his work be crowned with earthly success?

Jesus knew too accurately the hearts and minds of men to believe that inevitably they would accept and obey God's call to repent. Too well he had judged the innermost character of Sadducees, Pharisees, scribes, and of the common people to believe that they would quickly or easily accept his high, pure teaching from God. Men were blind and deaf; their hearts were hardened by long centuries of repeated, willful disobedience to God. The salvation of these men would be costly. Every demonic power in men and in the whole universe would be pitted savagely against him.

Jesus weighed realistically the cost of faithfulness to God and irrevocably dedicated his life to his Father in heaven; he accepted the threefold work of hallowing his Father's name, of bringing to men through his own life the reign of God, and of doing with loving obedience his Father's will, cost what it might. The Epistle to the Hebrews has caught clearly the characteristic note of Jesus' life, " Lo, I come to do thy will."

Here in the wilderness Jesus received and accepted from

God those principles that will at every step mark his ministry to men. Irrevocably he surrenders and dedicates his life to his Father, abandoning every claim upon God for personal safety or earthly success. Equally determined is Jesus that there can never be any equivalent or substitute for God's sole appointed way of entrance into the Kingdom — the way of repentance. Neither bread nor miracle will ever suffice to turn sinful men to God, and so receive the Kingdom.

Jesus has given us his temptation experiences under the imagery of a personal, evil being — Satan. We today are apt to depersonalize evil and we thereby lose sense of the *personal* conflict that is involved in all temptation. We would do well to follow unashamedly the wisdom of Jesus, and think of a great and widespread kingdom of evil wills, both human and cosmic, which seeks day and night to thwart and destroy the high and holy purposes of God to save and redeem the world. The siege of temptation is subtle and persistent, clever and intelligent; and we can rightly infer that behind it are evil wills that are at least personal. We, in the experience of temptation, are not dealing with impersonal, evil powers, but rather with intelligent, personal beings.

Still one further observation is forthcoming from the wilderness experiences of Jesus. The stories reveal to us that his mind and heart were saturated with the words of God, found in the Holy Scriptures. In every temptation it is not his own words, but the scriptural words of God that become his armor and defense. We can rightly surmise that from early childhood Joseph and Mary had ingrafted the words of God into his sensitive, receptive, and obedient mind. Years of humble schooling at the feet of some rabbi at Nazareth and habitual sabbath worship in the synagogue had implanted and nourished the words of God in him. Now in the time of conflict against evil these same words bring their rich harvest. Can we do better than to follow his practice here?

PART TWO

THE GALILEAN MINISTRY

3 GOD'S FIRST WORD – REPENTANCE

Now after that John was put in prison, Jesus came into Galilee, preaching the gospel of the kingdom of God, and saying, The time is fulfilled, and the kingdom of God is at hand: repent ye, and believe the gospel.

Mark 1: 14-15

Jesus' first word from God to men was *repent*. Such is still God's first word to every individual, every nation, every church. We cannot but look ahead to a later saying of Jesus, "Woe unto thee, Chorazin! woe unto thee, Bethsaida! for if the mighty works, which were done in you, had been done in Tyre and Sidon, they would have repented long ago." Nor will we today repent. The one thing that is the essential precondition for understanding and accepting the teaching and life of Jesus we *will* not do.

Jesus' first word is not bread and it is not miracle. Nor is it the forming of an organization and the drawing up of a plan by a committee. Rather it is the clear, unmistakable call to each individual person to repent, to turn to God. If his first word had been bread or miracle or scheme, then men could have debated and argued. But you cannot argue or debate the call to repent. Repentance is a call, not to the intellect alone, but to the heart and will also, a call to the whole man. We can say "Yes," or we can say "No"; but the question is not debatable.

4 JESUS CALLS FOUR DISCIPLES

Now as he walked by the sea of Galilee, he saw Simon and Andrew his brother casting a net into the sea: for they were fishers. And Jesus said unto them, Come ye after me, and I will make you to become fishers of men. And straightway they forsook their nets, and followed him.

11

And when he had gone a little farther thence, he saw James the son of Zebedee, and John his brother, who also were in the ship mending their nets. And straightway he called them: and they left their father Zebedee in the ship with the hired servants, and went after him.

Mark 1: 16-20

The ministry of Jesus is closely synchronized with two crises in the life of John the Baptist — his imprisonment and his death. Rightly has John been called the forerunner of Jesus. Already when Jesus began his public ministry, the people of Galilee had heard John's call to repentance through baptism.

No sooner is John's prophetic voice silenced by imprisonment than it is taken up by one who is far greater than John. By all rules of human expediency we should have expected Jesus to have chosen some other locality in which to begin his ministry than that of King Herod. The voice of a courageous and out-spoken prophet had just been silenced by Herod. It would then seem both tactless and foolhardy for Jesus to begin his work at that particular time and in territory belonging to Herod. We shall never be able to understand the course of Jesus' ministry, if we judge it on the basis of human expediency. The determining factor in his life and work is never the weigh-ing of the probable chances of earthly success, but solely obedience to the revealed will of God.

It is significant that Jesus' work was not to begin or finish by being subordinate to the religious leaders of Judaism — the Sadducees, the scribes, or the Pharisees. Instead it begins with the choosing of a few simple, unimposing men of Galilee. The ways of God are certainly not the ways of men. Always in God's way there is the note of unpredictability, amazement, and surprise. Paul will write truly that " the foolishness of God is wiser than men."

Throughout the remainder of their lives Simon and Andrew, James and John, must have looked back with wonder and amazement upon this event. Our earliest gospel records know nothing of any previous acquaintance of these fisherfolk with either John the Baptist or with Jesus. On that day when Jesus suddenly appeared at Capernaum and called them to follow him, they obeyed, but not because they knew who he was. Rather they obeyed, not knowing why. So it is today, as Jesus calls us to follow him. At the time of calling we know not who he is; only after years of discipleship do we grow into the realization of who he is.

This event portrays Jesus as from the very first exercising a strange and compelling power and authority over men. This is the first record in the Gospels of the mysterious and powerful impact which Jesus made upon men. The initial experience of the first four disciples in relation to Jesus was that of a person who commands with irresistible authority. What man is this?

Little could they then envisage what lay ahead for them. For James it would mean, only a very few years later, a martyr's death at Jerusalem. For Peter, some thirty years later, it would mean death by crucifixion at Rome. They followed Jesus, not knowing why they did so and not yet knowing who Jesus was.

Simon and Andrew, James and John — these are not the men whom we should have chosen to be the leaders and pillars of the new Church of God. All four men are of simple, middle-class folk; none of them were highly educated, having probably at best a simple synagogue education. None of them were men of refinement or culture. These four were rough fishermen, accustomed to deal with the elemental realities of human life.

Jesus chose them not for what they already were, but rather for what they could and would become under his powerful and loving impact upon them. "I will fashion you into fishers of men." They will become under Jesus' creative influence very different men than they now are. They will truly become *new* men in Jesus. Their main function will be not to reason or theologize, but to witness. Christian history has substantiated the wisdom of Jesus in choosing them. At least three of these four became martyr witnesses for Jesus as the Christ of God.

5 CASTING OUT AN UNCLEAN SPIRIT

They went into Capernaum; and straightway on the sabbath day he entered into the synagogue and taught. And they were astonished at his doctrine: for he taught them as one that had authority, and not as the scribes.

And there was in their synagogue a man with an unclean spirit; and he cried out, saying, Let us alone; what have we to do with thee, thou Jesus of Nazareth? art thou come to destroy us? I know thee who thou art, the Holy One of God. And Jesus rebuked him, saying, Hold thy peace, and come out of him.

And when the unclean spirit had torn him, and cried with a loud voice, he came out of him. And they were all amazed, insomuch that they questioned among themselves, saying, What thing is this? what new teaching is this? for with authority commandeth he even the unclean spirits, and they do obey him. And immediately his fame spread abroad throughout all the region round about Galilee.

Mark 1: 21-28

We are not told by Mark what Jesus taught, but we can rightly presume that it could only be based on one theme — the kingdom of God, and of entering into that kingdom by repentance. Instead we are told by very simple but profound artistry of the impression that Jesus' teaching made upon the hearers. This man taught them as no other teacher they had ever known. This man's wisdom gave the sure impression that it stemmed from God, and not at all from the schooling of men or writings. His teaching had a simplicity and directness which set it apart from all merely academic, theoretic knowledge. This teaching was alive. This teacher spoke of that which he knew at first hand.

At the very beginning of his public ministry, Jesus thus stood in the line and succession of the prophets, rather than of the scribes. The people of Galilee will think of Jesus as being " one of the prophets." Only very slowly will they come to realize that Jesus was more than a prophet.

Here is the first recorded miracle or mighty work of Jesus' ministry, and it again reveals him as being a unique person.

The demon, who had possession of this unfortunate man, was enabled (we know not how) to discern who Jesus was — " the Holy One of God." But with Jesus' terse command the demonic voice is silenced and the secret of Jesus' person is kept hidden. Who would give serious heed to the outcries of a demented, crazy man?

Jesus was determined that his true identity as the Messiah or Christ of God should not be revealed to any, not even to the chosen disciples, until the time appointed by God. It will not be until the Transfiguration that the secret will be disclosed, and then not by Jesus himself, but by the voice of God.

This miracle reveals to us something of the amazing faith and certainty of Jesus concerning the action of God in and through him. There is no use made of any magic rite of exorcism; there is no hesitant experiment to see if he can cast out the demon. Instead there is the calm, sure, confident, terse command: " Come out." Jesus, with no doubt at all, expects that God will instantly act through his words. The words of Jesus actually carry and transmit the healing power of God. Who is this man, who can so confidently command even demons, and expect that God will at once act through him to accomplish his command?

Jesus' deep and full assurance that God will surely act through his words is at once confirmed by the result. The demon left the man and he was healed. We can readily appreciate the reaction of the onlookers: " What thing is this? What new teaching is this? for with authority commandeth he even the unclean spirits, and they do obey him."

6 HEALINGS IN CAPERNAUM

Forthwith, when they were come out of the synagogue, they entered into the house of Simon and Andrew, with James and John. But Simon's wife's mother lay sick of a fever; and anon they tell him of her. And he came and took her by the hand, and lifted her up; and immediately the fever left her, and she ministered unto them.

And at even, when the sun did set, they brought unto him all that were diseased, and them that were possessed with devils. And all the city was gathered together at the door. And he healed many that were sick of divers diseases, and cast out many devils; and suffered not the devils to speak, because they knew him.

Mark 1: 29-34

This event is the immediate sequel to the sabbath-day healing in the synagogue. In Simon's home there lay sick the mother of his wife, and Jesus healed her. Jesus shows us that health and strength can be transferred from one life to another under God. Perhaps nothing is more mysterious and yet more undeniable than the power of one life to enter into the life of another and affect it for good or for ill. Here we have the method so often to be used by Jesus in his ministry — the method of touch or contact. By the outstretched hand of Jesus health and strength from God actually pass over to the woman — a spiritual trans-fusion, comparable to the better known blood transfusion. Jesus' life and ministry is marked, from beginning to end, by his unceasing, continual self-giving that others might live by him and from him.

The Jewish sabbath would end at sundown. Until that hour the people of Capernaum must remain bound by the legalism of the sabbath-day laws. But when the sabbath day had reached its close, the people at once hurried to the home of Simon and Andrew, bringing with them their sick and demonized folk. What an opportunity this afforded them of getting, and getting freely, the healing power of this man, who had such power over demons as had been manifested that morning in the synagogue.

We can picture in our imagination the quiet, unhurried, courteous, compassionate attention that Jesus gave to each of the sick. But the sequel to this eventful day will hold for us an unpredictable surprise.

7 JESUS AT PRAYER

In the morning, rising up a great while before day, he went out, and departed into a solitary place, and there prayed. And Simon and they that were with him followed after him. And when they had found him, they said unto him, All men seek for thee. And he said unto them, Let us go into the next towns, that I may preach there also: for therefore came I forth. And he preached in their synagogues throughout all Galilee, and cast out devils.

Mark 1: 35-39

In the gospel records we are given only a few terse accounts of Jesus' own life of prayer, but those few accounts are invariably associated with important crises in his ministry, moments when far-reaching decisions were made.

Jesus and his four disciples react in very different ways to the events of the preceding sabbath day. For the disciples, popularity and success were all that could be asked for. This would have been a ministry such as they would have welcomed.

With Jesus it was very different. He read so much more deeply and truly the hearts and motivations of men. His primary and central concern was that these people of Capernaum should receive from God the priceless gift of godly fellowship — eternal life. The precondition for receiving that gift from God was repentance. Would the mere fact of the physical cure of their diseases inevitably lead those cured to repentance? Do those, who today are released from hospitals, healed of their sicknesses, live therefore and thereafter more closely to God? Men will always be ready and eager to *use* God to get what they desire. But will they surrender their lives to God's sovereignty, when it involves repentance?

Jesus knew that there would be no end to the number of Galileans who would follow after him to be cured of their maladies, physical and mental. But what was this but the wilderness temptation in a new guise? Would these same people repent and turn to God and receive the kingdom? God had sent Jesus to preach and proclaim the kingdom of God. Healings were secondary, not primary. Healings he will do out of his never-failing compassion, but more and more he will seek to do them in secrecy. His primary work was to proclaim the kingdom of God, and to call men to enter into that kingdom through the lowly door of repentance. Shall he give men that which they desire and ask for, or that which God wills for them? Unswervingly Jesus remains faithful to the orders given him in the wilderness days.

8 HEALING A LEPER

There came a leper to him, beseeching him, and kneeling down to him, and saying unto him, If thou art willing, thou canst make me clean. And Jesus, moved with compassion, put forth his hand, and touched him, and saith unto him, I am willing; be thou clean. And as soon as he had spoken, immediately the leprosy departed from him, and he was cleansed. And he straitly charged him, . . . See thou say nothing to any man: but go thy way, show thyself to the priest, and offer for thy cleansing those things which Moses commanded, for a testimony unto them.

But he went out, and began to publish it much, and to blaze abroad the matter, insomuch that Jesus could no more openly enter into the city, but was without in desert places: and they came to him from every quarter.

Mark 1: 40-45

We cannot be sure that in this particular case the man had what we today call leprosy. We know today that sometimes leprosy may be cured with medicine. With them in that age true leprosy was not curable. It is to be presumed, therefore, since the Jewish law made provision for the cleansing of a leper and since Jesus bade the man report to the priests at Jerusalem for a declaration of his cure, that this was rather a case of infectious skin disease, commonly called leprosy.

During the very last week of Jesus' ministry we shall find him dining in the home of one Simon, a leper, at Bethany. To be living at home and entertaining Jesus, Simon's leprosy must have been cured. Reverent imagination would lead us to relate that incident with this event in Galilee.

To have an infectious skin disease involved isolation often from home, family, and community life. Moreover it involved in fact exclusion from all religious fellowship, whether in synagogue or temple. It is only a very short step from that earthly exclusion to believing that one is also shut out from fellowship with God. How can one believe in the companionship and compassion of God, when the people and servants of God exclude one from their presence? By Jewish law the infectious man was bound to observe the very strictest injunctions, which involved keeping at a safe distance from all other people.

It is noteworthy that this diseased man dared, on the basis of his faith in the power of this man Jesus to heal him, to break the Jewish injunctions concerning his infection. He drew so near to Jesus that he could be touched by his outstretched hand. Had he heard some rumor of the many healings by Jesus on the recent day in Capernaum? This Jesus was reputed to have a strange and unique power to heal men of their many diseases. Might he not also have power to heal him of his infection? But would this healer dare to touch his infectious body? Would he not turn away in loathing and fear, lest he himself become unclean? His cry indicates that he doubts not the power, but only the willingness of Jesus to heal him. "If thou art willing, thou canst make me clean."

That a man could believe that he had the power, but was unwilling to heal him, was a thought which was abhorrent to Jesus. He knew that the power to heal this man issued, not from himself, but from God. The healing power came through him, but not from him. Ultimately, although the man knew it not, his doubt was a doubt concerning the will in God to heal. Jesus was filled with deep compassion at the horrible and tragic misbelief of the leper concerning God.

Jesus feared no contagion for himself. If he had, he would

have healed him simply by a word. But in that case the leper, with his already expressed doubt of Jesus' willingness to heal him, would have no tangible assurance that Jesus *did* will to cure him. That he might have full and certain assurance, Jesus places his hand upon the leper, and at once the healing, cleansing, loving power of God flows into the man, and he is cured of his infectious disease. Who is this man Jesus, who can so confidently undertake this daring act?

We can well understand Jesus' desire not to have this tremendous miracle publicized. We can equally well understand why the cured man disobeyed him. Here was something far too wondrous and amazing to be kept secret. And why make the long journey to Jerusalem to consult a priest, when he himself knew he was cleansed? No pronouncement of any priest would add anything to his knowledge that he was cured.

Paradoxically, the cured man, who formerly was isolated from society, is now restored to human fellowship and community life; whereas Jesus, because of fast-spreading fame, is now compelled to live apart from the cities and towns of Galilee. Even so, Jesus is sought out by the crowds of eager, expectant people of the whole region.

9 A PARALYTIC AND FORGIVENESS

Again he entered into Capernaum after some days; and it was noised that he was in the house. And straightway many were gathered together, insomuch that there was no room to receive them, no, not so much as about the door: and he preached the word unto them.

And they come unto him, bringing one sick of the palsy, which was borne of four. And when they could not come nigh unto him for the press, they uncovered the roof where he was: and when they had broken it up, they let down the bed wherein the sick of the palsy lay. When Jesus saw their faith, he said unto the sick of the palsy, Son, thy sins be forgiven thee.

But there were certain of the scribes sitting there, and reasoning in their hearts, Why doth this man thus speak blasphemies? who can forgive sins but God only? And immediately, when Jesus perceived in his spirit that they so reasoned within themselves, he said unto them, Why reason ye these things in your hearts? Whether is it easier to say to the sick of the palsy, Thy sins be forgiven thee; or to say, Arise, and take up thy bed, and walk? But that ye may know that the Son of Man hath power on earth to forgive sins, (he saith to the sick of the palsy,) I say unto thee, Arise, and take up thy bed, and go thy way into thine house. And immediately he arose, took up the bed, and went forth before them all; insomuch that they were all amazed, and glorified God, saying, We never saw it on this fashion.

Mark 2: 1-12

That this incident was counted by the early church as of central importance is evidenced vividly from the art symbols which the church used. Among them is commonly found the crudely drawn outline of a man, carrying a bedding roll on his shoulder. Why did the early Christians select this incident out of the many in Jesus' ministry for their especial concern? Was it not because they knew that the very core and heart of the Christian experience of God through Jesus was forgiveness? The early chapters of the Acts of the Apostles, as also the letters of Paul, stress the note of forgiveness as being central in the Christian faith.

Here is an act of forgiveness utterly unparalleled in Jewish teaching or practice. Pharisaic teaching was that God forgives only on the basis of strict and onerous conditions. When a man has made himself repentant and ceased to be a sinner and has met the demands of the law, then and then only will God forgive him and restore him to his fellowship. But in this act of Jesus we have unmistakably a case of forgiveness preceding any repentance. At the close of his ministry, while hanging upon the cross, we shall again meet Jesus forgiving in the total absence of any repentance, as he prays, " Father, forgive them; for they know not what they do." Paul will write in one of his letters that it is " the goodness of God " which " leadeth thee to repentance."

Man's experience of repentance and forgiveness does not have its origin in himself, but in the prevenience of God. Our repentance does not begin God's forgiveness. Rather it marks the point in the long process of God's forgiving work, when we are called upon by God to take a co-operative role in the work of our remaking. God begins the work of forgiveness long before we awaken to his work, while we are still sinful, blinded and deafened from our sin, and thus unable to see it in true perspective. Only late in the whole process of re-creation does the sinner awaken to God's judgment and to the work that God has already accomplished. In the experience of repentance God calls upon us to acknowledge our sin, and to give him thanks for that which he has already done in us, and to surrender freely and fully our wills to his for the completion of the mighty work of forgiveness.

We are now ready to consider the event itself. A paralyzed man is carried to Jesus by four friends, who had faith and hope that he could heal their friend. We are in no way given any evidence that the four friends are vicariously repentant on be-half of their sick friend. It may even have been that their moti-vation was a selfish one — their desire that this man be healed so that he and his family no longer will be a burden to them. God is willing, in his great humility and lowly love, to be approached with low and selfish motives. But slowly and imperceptibly God transmutes motivations and we finally awaken to our selfish use of him.

It is not the faith of the paralytic, but of the four friends, that Jesus sees. The paralytic apparently had none. We need to be very careful not to suppose that the faith of the four friends is faith in Jesus as the " Son of God." Nobody even suspects that he is that, except a few demented persons; and who would give any credence to their insane cries? Their faith is simply faith in Jesus as a man possessing unusual healing powers.

Jesus read deeply and accurately the hearts of men. He read them far more truly than men could read their own hearts. We, the sinful, with the blindness and deafness that are the invariable consequences of our past sinning, can hardly begin even to comprehend the certitude of vision which would result from a life of total purity and unswerving obedience to God. Jesus' vision was in no way marred or blurred by sin, as is ours. He read at once the deep, inarticulate, unuttered need of the paralytic. His four friends might in deep sincerity think that all that the paralytic needed or wanted was to walk again. If only he could walk, then all would be well with him.

Jesus, however, saw that even though this man should walk again, there would still remain within him the heavy burden which was the cause of the physical paralysis — sin unforgiven. This man could not forget the hideous and loathsome sin which he had committed, that sin for which there could never be an undoing or an atonement. Forgiveness for that which he had done seemed so utterly impossible that he had even ceased to hope for it. But Jesus was wont to give better and greater things than men hoped or asked. The four friends ask for physical healing. The paralytic himself asked for nothing. Jesus gave first of all that for which none of them had asked — forgiveness. Only when that was given, was there given in addition physical healing.

The heart of forgiveness, on our human side, is release from the enslaving loneliness that issues from all sinning and entrance into a new kind of companionship with God through Jesus, a relationship in which we are voluntarily and gladly surrendered to open and submissive obedience. Unless both of these aspects are operative on our human side, the forgiveness is sterile and impotent. On God's side forgiveness is his full, free giving of himself to us the sinful, in order that by his indwelling of us we may become new creatures.

Such was the deepest need of the paralytic, and into him there entered from God, through Jesus, the living power of forgiveness. In and through Jesus' words, God acts. Into the paralytic there flowed the healing, recreating life of God. At once the source of the physical paralysis is broken.

Quickly the scribes rise to the conflict. These words of Jesus were blasphemous. Who but God alone could forgive sins? Moreover, this was not the way in which God forgives. Where was the sign of this man's repentance? His very paralysis was vivid evidence that God's wrath was upon him. Who does this Jesus presume to be, thus to pronounce the forgiveness of God upon this sinner?

In Jesus' reply to their complaint we are given a glimpse into his own self-consciousness. True, only God can forgive sins. But Jesus, in and through his unique relationship with God, had authority from God to proclaim and to transmit God's own forgiving love. The forgiveness which he pronounced was not simply his own human forgiveness, but that of God. It is as if Jesus said, "I forgive; yet not I, but God forgives in and through me."

Jesus had no doubt as to the validity of his diagnosis, nor of God's instantaneous working through his words. Without any hesitation, and as proof both to the paralytic and to the scribes, Jesus commanded the man to rise up, take up his bed, and walk. And he did it. Who is this man Jesus, who so confidently can speak the word, and have his words at once confirmed by a mighty action of God? One of the charges later directed against Jesus was that he presumed blasphemously to forgive sins, a prerogative belonging exclusively to God. Wherever the Christian faith has been carried, it has proclaimed the good news of free, unmerited, unconditional, prevenient forgiveness of God through Jesus.

10 THE CALLING OF MATTHEW AND THE CRITICISM THAT FOLLOWED

Jesus went forth again by the sea side; and all the multitude resorted unto him, and he taught them. And as he passed by, he saw Levi, the son of Alphaeus, sitting at the receipt of custom, and said unto him, Follow me. And he arose and followed him.

And it came to pass, that, as Jesus sat at meat in his house, many publicans and sinners sat also together with Jesus and his disciples: for there were many, and they followed him. And when the scribes and Pharisees saw him eat with publicans and sinners, they said unto his disciples, How is it that he eateth and drinketh with publicans and sinners? When Jesus heard it, he saith unto them, They that are whole have no need of the physician, but they that are sick: I came not to call the righteous, but sinners to repentance.

Mark 2: 13-17

This act of Jesus will quickly bring upon himself the open hostility of the righteous Jews of Capernaum. Levi, whom we know better by the name of Matthew, was a Jew who had undertaken to serve the exploiting and domineering Roman Empire as a tax collector. It was hard enough for Jews to be compelled to tolerate Roman military and economic enslavement, but it was quite unbearable to have to accept a fellow Jew voluntarily serving Rome. We presume therefore that Levi was a religious outcast, for all practical purposes excommunicate from the synagogue. No righteous Jew would voluntarily have any dealings with him. Matthew must have been a very lonely man.

Why Jesus chose Matthew, the gospel records do not tell us. Certainly he was not chosen for reasons of human expediency. Nothing could have been more inexpedient or unfitting than Jesus' choice of a despised and hated Jewish traitor. This act of Jesus does not fit into any of the normal patterns of human behavior.

With this choosing of Matthew, Jesus is at once confronted with the open opposition and deep scorn of the religious leaders of Capernaum. One of the taunts which will be directed against him is that he was "a friend of publicans and sinners." Later in his ministry we shall find Jesus befriending another publican outcast, Zacchaeus of Jericho; and we naturally suppose that Matthew had a leading part to play in preparing Zacchaeus for that encounter with Jesus.

Matthew immediately confirms Jesus' wisdom in choosing him. He at once brings together for a feast in his home a number of fellow publicans and sinners, i.e., those who, although Jews, did not attend the synagogues. Matthew wanted them to meet and know Jesus, who had so befriended and honored him by calling him to be one of his chosen disciples.

In the small town of Capernaum nothing could be hidden, and we can readily imagine that tongues wagged fast and furiously over what was taking place in Matthew's home. "How is it that he eateth and drinketh with publicans and sinners? " These are words filled with scorn for Jesus. Yet how courteously Jesus responds to the critics' bitter attitude towards him. Jesus can rebuke, but always his rebukes are administered in love.

Those who count themselves righteous, measuring themselves by themselves or in comparison with others worse than themselves, cannot repent. They know not the hollowness and hypocrisy of their own self-judgments. But sinners are under no illusion as to their true condition. They know their own sinfulness against God, and their comparative unworthiness. It is for such that Jesus has come from God. Jesus' judgment of his own life is that he has been sent from God to sinners to call them to repentance.

11 TEACHING CONCERNING FASTING

The disciples of John and of the Pharisees used to fast: and they come and say unto him, Why do the disciples of John and of the Pharisees fast, but thy disciples fast not? And Jesus said unto them, Can the children of the bridechamber fast, while the bridegroom is with them? as long as they have the bridegroom with them, they cannot fast. But the days will come, when the bridegroom shall be taken away from them, and then shall they fast in those days.

Mark 2: 18-20

Nowhere else in the New Testament are we given such definite and authoritative teaching from Jesus concerning fasting. Christians today need a clear understanding concerning this practice of religion. This teaching came from Jesus, who himself fasted in the wilderness.

Fasting with Jesus was never a meritorious, self-seeking, religious exercise. His fasting rather resulted naturally and necessarily from the immediate occasion, and never from mere obedience to a code of religious self-discipline. His fasting is not to be compared with that of the Pharisees who, when they fast, " disfigure their faces, that they may appear unto men to fast." Jesus' fasting was the natural and fitting accompaniment to his all-absorbing concern for the things of God. Undoubtedly it never occurred to Jesus that he was fasting.

This — Jesus teaches — is no place or time for fasting, when he is giving his authoritative and new teaching concerning the reign of God and performing his compassionate acts of healing. To fast under these conditions would be an artificial religious exercise as unfitting as having a long and sad countenance at a wedding feast.

" But the time will come. . . ." Is this still another glimpse into the inner consciousness of Jesus, still another self-disclosure of his coming fate on the cross? Jesus knew too well the hearts of men to believe that even God's own people would repent and accept God's call to radical remaking. Repentance must be born, not from his teaching, but from his death and resurrection. In those three days immediately following Gethsemane his disciples would truly and literally fast. Then their fasting will be something far deeper and more significant than a religious exercise. In those days they will have no heart, no desire to eat anything. Their fasting will be born out of their anguish and despair and will be a fasting acceptable before God. But after the experience of Easter, again fasting will be out of place and unfitting, supplanted entirely by joy and thankfulness. Christian fasting must forever have about it a unique quality and significance, distinguishing it from merely ceremonial fasting.

12 PATCHES AND WINE

No man also seweth a piece of new cloth on an old garment: else the new piece that filled it up taketh away from the old, and the rent is made worse.

And no man putteth new wine into old wine-skins; else the new wine will burst the wine-skins, and be spilled, and the wine-skins shall perish. But new wine must be put into new wine-skins; and both are preserved. No man also having drunk old wine straightway desireth new: for he saith, The old is better.

Mark 2: 21 and Luke 5: 37-39

In these two vivid, unforgettable analogies Jesus gives us his own estimate concerning his teaching. He knew that his teaching was new. It could not be fitted harmoniously into the traditional religious patterns of Judaism. Our own age has tended to overlook the radical opposition between the *old* and the *new* relationships with God, so much so that we are hard put to it in understanding why there was such a bitter conflict between the two faiths in those early centuries. We forget or are still unawakened to the truth that in Jesus there has been given to men a *New Testament*, a *new* life with God, which the Old Testament of the Law could never give. Early Christian history abundantly witnesses to the truth of Jesus' own estimate that there must come an inevitable rent or schism between a faith based upon the Law and that based upon the person of Jesus.

We today can readily grasp how a patch of new cloth cannot harmonize with an old, worn piece of clothing. But with the analogy of wine and wineskins, just because we are accustomed to put wine into bottles and not skins, we require to be made familiar with a Palestinian custom. They placed new, un-fermented wine into new lambskins. Skins which had been used previously, because of the powerful action of fermentation, had become stretched and expanded to capacity. If new, fermenting wine were placed in used skins, the skins would soon burst and the wine would thus be lost.

Jesus counts his own teaching concerning God as new, fermenting wine. Invisibly but powerfully his doctrine would ferment, and if placed in the old Jewish religious containers, would burst them. The religious conceptions of Judaism had already expanded and hardened to their full capacity. They could not stand the life and power of this new teaching of Jesus. The new containers for the Christian faith were not to be either the temple priesthood, nor the Pharisees with their Law. Instead, the containers will be the little apostolic band of disciples, who will be the witnesses of his resurrection.

In this analogy Jesus also recognizes the power of tradition. The new religious thought forms will certainly arouse violent opposition from those who, through long years, have become rigidly accustomed to the old. Only a few, brave, adventure-some persons will dare to accept the hidden implications of Jesus' teaching and follow where it will lead — notably Stephen, Philip, and Paul.

13 SABBATH-DAY LAWS

It came to pass, that he went through the corn fields on the sabbath day; and his disciples began, as they went, to pluck the ears of corn. And the Pharisees said unto him, Behold, why do they on the sabbath day that which is not lawful? And he said unto them, Have ye never read what David did, when he had need, and was anhungred, he, and they that were with him? How he went into the house of God in the days of Abiathar the high priest, and did eat the shewbread, which is not lawful to eat but for the priests, and gave also to them which were with him? And he said unto them, The sabbath was made for man, and not man for the sabbath: Therefore the Son of Man is Lord also of the sabbath.

Mark 2: 23-28

A constant danger confronting all religion is that its demands be interpreted in a legalistic manner, and that judgments be formed on the basis of merely external actions. Legalistic religion so easily overlooks interior motivations, in its major concern for external actions. It asks not, Why did he do this? but only, Did he do this? True, from the perspective of legalism, Jesus' disciples had trespassed against the Law. But Jesus, both by teaching and action, breaks the externalism of the Law, and insists upon shifting the perspective to that of inner motivation. He knew from long familiarity the Holy Scriptures of his people. There was the clear case where David, faced with pressing need, did not hesitate to break another religious injunction — to take and eat holy bread, which only the temple priests were permitted to eat.

The sabbath-day laws were in their origin motivated by the desire to help man remember God; but through the many centuries they had become rigid shackles, and no longer were serving God's purposes. Man's basic needs — here hunger — are ever to take precedence over merely ritual commandments.

14 HEALING ON THE SABBATH

He entered again into the synagogue; and there was a man there which had a withered hand. And they watched him, whether he would heal him on the sabbath day; that they might accuse him.

And he saith unto the man which had the withered hand, Stand forth. And he saith unto them, Is it lawful to do good on the sabbath days, or to do evil? to save life, or to kill? But they held their peace. And when he had looked round about on them with anger, being grieved for the hardness of their hearts, he saith unto the man, Stretch forth thine hand. And he stretched it out: and his hand was restored whole as the other.

And the Pharisees went forth, and straightway took counsel with the Herodians against him, how they might destroy him.

Mark 3: 1-6

Jesus' challenge to the Pharisees concerning the sabbath-day laws in the previous event is the background for this new event.

The former occasion was perhaps unpremeditated; this one sounds like a set trap.

This was no emergency case, requiring healing on that particular day. The man with the withered hand well might have waited until the next day, when there would have been no occasion for breaking any laws. We suspect, therefore, that the crippled man was there, perhaps unknowingly to himself, at the instigation of the enemies of Jesus, to be used by them for their subtle purposes of trapping Jesus. Mark records that in the synagogue they were watching Jesus critically, that they might find a cause for attacking him. Such was hardly the right motivation for attending synagogue worship, or one which would be acceptable to God.

All through the gospel records of Jesus' ministry we find him reading unerringly the hearts and minds of men. He read on this occasion their stares, for their faces could not hide from his keen eyes their dispositions. Jesus at once accepts their challenge, but nobody but Jesus could have done it in so courteous a way. He does it in such a fashion that none of them *need* feel the sting of defeat. He raises the issue from one of literal, external legalism, i.e., breaking the letter of the sabbath laws, to a new and higher level, where the only possible answer is clear and unequivocal. Is it legal to do good on the sabbath days? There is but one reply possible to that question.

The tragedy of this event is that the Pharisees would not give the only logical, natural answer to Jesus' question. They refused to answer him. They could hardly answer with a "No"; and they *would not* reply "Yes."

Therefore Jesus looked round about on them with anger, as he in silence gazed into each pair of eyes. The silent look from Jesus' eyes spoke louder than any words which his lips might have pronounced. But even Jesus' anger is courteous. Here is no mild, gentle, tolerant, condoning Jesus, but a righteous, all-searching Jesus. They themselves were not grieved or troubled at their own hardness of heart; but Jesus was grieved for them vicariously. Throughout the entire Bible runs this constant theme, ever re-echoed in myriad forms — the hardness of men's hearts.

Jesus gave them the answer they would not utter themselves — in the form of an action. "Stretch forth thine hand." In those words healing power from God leaped into instantaneous action, bringing to the amazed cripple the restoration of his withered hand.

"Is it lawful to do evil on the sabbath days?" That is the other side of Jesus' question to the Pharisees. That Jesus read accurately their hearts is evidenced by the immediate sequel. The Pharisees went forth from the worship of God to plot with the Herodians (the political-minded party of Jews in Galilee) the death of this man. Legalistic religion always blinds. Future events will reveal how the plot, here begun, will be carried to its full fruition upon the cross on Calvary.

15 WITHDRAWAL FROM THE SYNAGOGUES

But Jesus withdrew himself with his disciples to the sea: and a great multitude from Galilee followed him, and from Judea, and from Jerusalem, and from Idumea, and from beyond Jordan; and they about Tyre and Sidon, a great multitude, when they heard what great things he did, came unto him.

And he spake to his disciples, that a small ship should wait on him because of the multitude, lest they should throng him. For he had healed many; insomuch that they pressed upon him for to touch him, as many as had plagues. And unclean spirits, when they saw him, fell down before him, and cried, saying, Thou art the Son of God. And he straitly charged them that they should not make him known.

Mark 3: 7-12

That Jesus had to withdraw with his disciples to the seaside follows quite naturally from the previous event. From this time forth Jesus was for all practical purposes excommunicate from the synagogues, to be literally one of those whom the superior Pharisees derisively called "sinners."

In any event the little synagogue at Capernaum was now far too small to accommodate the crowds of people who came to see and hear Jesus. Mark records the vast geographical region from which the people came to be with Jesus. Even out of doors by the seaside the throng was so heavy that Jesus had to utilize a small boat (presumably one belonging to Peter and Andrew); and from that vantage point Jesus taught the multitudes on the beach. We can well picture the jealousy and bitterness of the synagogue leaders as they saw the crowds follow Jesus.

16 CHOOSING TWELVE DISCIPLES

He goeth up into a mountain, and calleth unto him whom he would: and they came unto him. And he ordained twelve, that they should be with him, and that he might send them forth to preach, and to have power to heal sicknesses, and to cast out devils: and Simon he surnamed Peter; and James the son of Zebedee, and John the brother of James; and he surnamed them Boanerges, which is The sons of thunder: and Andrew, and Philip, and Bartholomew, and Matthew, and Thomas, and James the son of Alphaeus, and Thaddaeus, and Simon the Canaanite, and Judas Iscariot, which also betrayed him.

Mark 3: 13-19

Whenever we find Jesus retiring from the crowds, often to the isolation and quiet of some mountain side, we can be sure that a decisive moment in his ministry is at hand. The yeast of the Pharisees is already working, although time will be required for it to do its work.

Jesus chose twelve men and ordained them, that they should be with him. The initiative is with Jesus, not with the disciples. It is not that they volunteer on their own impulse, and that then he accepts them. Rather it is he who calls them, and their part is to accept and obey.

To ordain is to prepare, to equip, to rule, to set in order. The Gospels are entirely silent concerning the reasons for Jesus' choice of these twelve men. We are left with the deep mystery of his choosing. By the time that the Gospels were written it had become abundantly clear that Jesus had chosen these twelve not for any personal qualifications which they already possessed. The memory of their unanimous forsaking of Jesus at the supreme crisis of his ministry would forever preclude any tradition of the worth of the twelve. The basis of choice lay in Jesus, not in them. So it is with all today who are called into the ministry of the risen Jesus. It is not because of what we already are that we have been called; rather it is for what Jesus will make of us, if we are willing and obedient. Our sufficiency is of Jesus, not of ourselves.

We may wish that we had reliable tradition concerning the lives and work of these twelve men after the resurrection. We know only a few scattered facts about a few of them — Simon Peter, James, and John. We can perhaps understand why this should be so. The writers of the Gospels were concerned to portray Jesus; every other figure had for them but peripheral interest.

17 BEELZEBUL

The scribes which came down from Jerusalem said, He hath Beelzebul, and by the prince of the devils casteth he out devils.

And he called them unto him, and said unto them in parables, How can Satan cast out Satan? And if a kingdom be divided against itself, that kingdom cannot stand. And if a house be divided against itself, that house cannot stand. And if Satan rise up against himself, and be divided, he cannot stand, but hath an end. No man can enter into a strong man's house, and spoil his goods, except he will first bind the strong man; and then he will spoil his house.

But if I with the finger of God cast out devils, no doubt the kingdom of God is come upon you.

Verily I say unto you, All sins shall be forgiven unto the sons of men, and blasphemies wherewith soever they shall blaspheme: but he that shall blaspheme against the Holy Ghost hath never forgiveness, but is in danger of eternal damnation.

Mark 3: 22-29 and Luke 11: 20

Our English texts should read Beelzebul,[1] and not Beelzebub. In 2 Kings 1: 2, 3, 16 we are told of one named Baalzebub, the particular local god worshiped at Ekron by the Philistines. Beelzebub is but the Aramaic corruption of that name, which meant " lord of flies." The name seems impossibly queer to us, but apparently it did not to those who were his worshipers. Any god who can rule the flies would be a very powerful god. The Jews looked upon this particular heathen god as the chief of all the pagan gods.

When the name is spelled however with a final " l " instead of a final " b," the word then takes on still another meaning — "lord of the dung." This was the foul epithet which the superior, elite scribes from Jerusalem used of Jesus to express their scorn and derision for him.

Jesus ignores the form of their charge against him and instead deals only with the substance of their complaint. That Matthew in his record of Jesus' life can record Jesus at a later time in his ministry as saying, " If they have called the master of the house Beelzebul " indicates that Jesus carried as a heavy burden this epithet of the scribes. The substance of the charge against Jesus was that he was doing his work of casting out demons from men, not by the power of God, but by the might of Satan. This charge Jesus quietly but directly corrects by using a parable.

First, and without any trace of rancor, he corrects their naming of the chief of the devils. The right name is neither Beelzebub nor Beelzebul, but Satan.

Then Jesus goes on to point out the absurdity of their diagnosis. Would Satan undo his own work? That would be ludicrous — Satan undoing the work of his own agents. Then Jesus gives us instead his own very different diagnosis. " No man can enter into a strong man's house, and spoil his goods,

---

[1] *Beelzebul* is used in the *New Testament in Modern Speech*, translated by Weymouth, and in *The Bible, a New Translation* by Moffatt.

except he will first bind the strong man." Jesus counted himself stronger than Satan. Who is this man who can dare to make such an astounding claim for himself?

Jesus goes further than this hint, for Luke records him as saying, "But if I with the finger of God cast out devils, no doubt the kingdom of God is come upon you." Here we are confronted with one of the most direct and high claims of Jesus in his whole ministry. Jesus counted his own acts of healing as being the works of God's own fingers. Jesus' hands were the hands of God. Through Jesus' acts the kingdom of God was breaking in upon men and freeing them from imprisonment to Satan.

Having dealt with the substance of the charge of his adversaries, Jesus then deals objectively and firmly with these Jerusalem scribes. Any man who can see the mighty deeds which Jesus has done, and can call them the deeds of Satan, is in a dire state of spiritual blindness. Such a man shuts himself out from the salvation which God seeks to bestow and is in danger of eternal banishment from the presence of God.

18 FAMILY OPPOSITION

. . . They went into an house. And the multitude cometh together again, so that they could not so much as eat bread.

And when his friends heard of it, they went out to lay hold on him: for they said, He is beside himself.

There came then his brethren and his mother, and, standing without, sent unto him, calling him. And the multitude sat about him, and they said unto him, Behold, thy mother and thy brethren without seek for thee. And he answered them, saying, Who is my mother, or my brethren? And he looked round about on them which sat about him, and said, Behold, my mother and my brethren! For whosoever shall do the will of God, the same is my brother, and my sister, and mother.

Mark 3: 19-21, 31-35

We have here our first inkling that the members of Jesus' own family were not with him, but opposed to his ministry.

It may have been that echoes of the mounting hostility of the Jewish religious leaders, not only of Galilee but also now of Jerusalem, had come to their ears. They were alarmed at the prospect of serious danger to one so close to them.

Our text here goes much further than this simple alarm of his kin for his personal safety. " He is beside himself." That means that his family believed him to be crazy; and they desired to protect Jesus, not only from his Pharisee enemies, but from himself.

The absence here of any reference to Joseph is probably an indication that he was at this time no longer living. Had he been still alive, it would have fallen to him to have invoked against Jesus the family power and will.

Jesus read unerringly the hearts and minds of his mother and brethren. Later he will teach his disciples that a man's foes are they of his own household, and that he came not to bring peace, but a sword into the family life. Yet, Jesus' answer to his family here is one filled to overflowing with courtesy and reverence. His words, " for whosoever shall do the will of God, the same is my brother, and my sister, and mother," in no way exclude the physical, natural, family relations. But loyal obedience to God takes precedence over every other loyalty, even that of the home. Nobody is shut out from this new and higher relationship, except by his own choice. Surely no more gentle but firm way could have been imagined in which to give the much needed rebuke to those of his own family, who unwittingly were seeking to call Jesus away from a ministry appointed him by God.

From this time forth, down to the end in Jerusalem, we have no evidence whatsoever of any of his family being in the rank of disciples or followers. Literally from this time on Jesus was a man without a home and could not count on family support or sympathy. Not until after the resurrection did his brother James come to believe in him.

19 THE PARABLE OF THE SOWER

He began again to teach by the sea side: and there was gathered unto him a great multitude, so that he entered into a ship, and sat in the sea; and the whole multitude was by the sea on the land.

And he taught them many things by parables, and said unto them in his teaching, Hearken; Behold, there went out a sower to sow: and it came to pass, as he sowed, some fell by the way side, and the fowls of the air came and devoured it up. And some fell on stony ground, where it had not much earth; and immediately it sprang up, because it had no depth of earth: but when the sun was up, it was scorched; and because it had no root, it withered away. And some fell among thorns, and the thorns grew up, and choked it, and it yielded no fruit. And other fell on good ground, and did yield fruit that sprang up and increased; and brought forth, some thirty, and some sixty, and some an hundred. And he said unto them, He that hath ears to hear, let him hear.

Mark 4: 1-9

We now come to a section in Mark's account of the gospel, dealing with the teaching of Jesus concerning the kingdom of God, given in the form of parables. A word of introduction therefore is in order.

By the time that Jesus' teachings were given written form, there existed a strong tendency to allegorize them. It was part of the temper of the age and even the Christian Church could not escape it entirely. In no case is this tendency more clearly seen than in the verses in Mark which follow this section. Jesus' solemn words, " He that hath ears to hear, let him hear," appear to be the conclusion of his teaching parable. The verses which follow in our English Bibles amount to a serious and radical change of perspective, from that of the sower of the seed to that of the various kinds of soils. The change marks the transformation of the parable into an allegory. Whereas in Jesus' parable the key figure is the sower, in the allegory which follows the center of interest is not at all the sower, but the receptivity of men, under the imagery of the various kinds of soil. Because our own age tends to place its religious focus in itself, rather than in God, and in our own inner, psychological

states, rather than in the work which God does, we are apt to
be unaware of the radical change.

Let us try then to understand the parable as a parable, not as
an allegory; and seek to understand it through the ears of
Jesus' first listeners. Jesus is seated in a boat, teaching the
crowds upon the beach. In the course of his teaching, Jesus
said, " Behold, there went out a sower to sow. . . ." It may have
been that Jesus actually pointed to some Galilean farmer engaged in sowing his seed.

We must rid our imaginations of our Western methods of
farming, so radically unlike those of the Orient. We use seeds
which have been carefully tested and protected against plant
diseases; we plant in drills or furrows; and we do not expect to
face any serious loss from non-germination. We expect that
a very large percentage of the seed will germinate and grow
into a harvest. It is very different with the oriental farmer.

Let us picture in our minds a barefooted farmer, striding
across his ploughed field in long, steady strides, holding in his
arm a tray or basket full of precious seed. As he goes across
his field, he takes great handfuls of seed and throws them upon
the soil. If it were a windy day, some of the light seed would
be carried by the wind to the sides of the field; birds would
follow behind and eat up much of the seed before it could be
covered. Much of the Galilean soil was shallow, and rock ledges
cropped up; seed falling in such places would germinate quickly,
but would also soon wither because of the inability of the roots
to find nourishment.

The key point to all of this was the fact that the farmer
expected a serious loss of seed. We are reminded of Psalm 126
with its verses, " They that sow in tears shall reap in joy. He
that goeth forth and weepeth, bearing precious seed. . . ."

We of the West are inclined to judge oriental farming as a
foolish, wasteful procedure. Jesus, however, saw in it a perfect
picture of God's dealings with men. The sower is apt imagery

for the prodigality of God. Jesus was here not concerned with men's receptivity, but instead with God's bounteous giving. His interest was theocentric, not anthropocentric.

God broadcasts his love in myriad forms. He does not carefully and coldly calculate the possibilities of success or the probability of a favorable response on man's part. We can never understand Jesus' ministry, if we judge it by the standards of probable, earthly success. God gives bounteously to all, regardless of whether men will accept or refuse his gifts. God continues unto the end to give lavishly and prodigally, even though he foresees that much of what he offers will be offered in vain and bring no return. Each of us knows that a very large measure of God's gifts to us has brought no fruit. We have taken his gifts for granted, misused and abused them, and often ignored them. Yet God still loves us. We also know that the gifts which we have accepted from his hands have borne fruit in amazing proportion.

20 THE KINGDOM OF GOD

And he said, So is the kingdom of God, as if a man should cast seed into the ground; and should sleep, and rise night and day, and the seed should spring and grow up, he knoweth not how. For the earth bringeth forth fruit of herself; first the blade, then the ear, after that the full corn in the ear. But when the fruit is brought forth, immediately he putteth in the sickle, because the harvest is come.

Mark 4: 26-29

Here again Jesus uses an analogy taken from the experience of farming. In the parable of the sower the key point was the lavish, bountiful sower scattering his seed, with full knowledge that a very large part of it would never bear any harvest. Here, however, the center of emphasis is upon the helplessness of man. While a man sleeps and rises night and day, occupying himself with other matters, the seed grows by itself, he knows not how. It grows without his help. It grows for him and not by him. Man's part is humbly to receive that which is done for him by the powers operating in nature — powers that come from God.

So, too, the kingdom of God is not brought into existence by man's own efforts and work. Rather one enters the kingdom because of the work that God himself does for us.

21 MUSTARD SEED

And he said, Whereunto shall we liken the kingdom of God? or with what comparison shall we compare it? It is like a grain of mustard seed, which, when it is sown in the earth, is less than all the seeds that be in the earth: but when it is sown, it groweth up, and becometh greater than all herbs, and shooteth out great branches; so that the fowls of the air may lodge under the shadow of it.

And with many such parables spake he the word unto them, as they were able to hear it.

Mark 4: 30-33

In this third parable based upon farming, the emphasis is upon the amazing contrast between the little beginning and the great end. The mustard seed, one of the smallest seeds known to antiquity, in one short season grows into a large bush, so large that birds may nest in the shadows of its branches. Such an astounding growth from so small a seed seems a marvel.

It is an apt imagery for the new fellowship which is being sown in the work of Jesus — Jesus, an obscure Galilean from a third-rate hill village, and twelve equally obscure followers from Galilee. Surely no one could have predicted that from that humble and mean beginning there would issue that new fellowship with God — the Christian Church.

Here Jesus' faith lies not in the seed, but in the growth which God will give to the seed which he is sowing. Although no other's faith could have envisaged such an end, yet Jesus' faith could and did.

22 A STORM AT SEA

The same day, when the even was come, he saith unto them, Let us pass over unto the other side. And when they had sent away the multitude, they took him even as he was in the ship. And there were also with him other little ships.

And there arose a great storm of wind, and the waves beat into the ship, so that it was now full. And he was in the hinder part of the ship, asleep on a pillow: and they awake him, and say unto him, Master, carest thou not that we perish? And he arose, and rebuked the wind, and said unto the sea, Peace, be still. And the wind ceased, and there was a great calm. And he said unto them, Why are ye so fearful? how is it that ye have no faith? And they feared exceedingly, and said one to another, What manner of man is this, that even the wind and the sea obey him?

Mark 4: 35-41

When we remember the temptation of Jesus in the wilderness and his rejection of the way of miracle to entice men into the kingdom of God, we shall then in this story center our attention not upon the mighty power of Jesus upon wind and waves, but rather upon the inner experiences of the disciples in relationship to Jesus.

At least four of the disciples were Galilean fisherfolk, with long years of experience with the storms which would suddenly sweep down from the hills upon the lake, and just as suddenly cease. This particular storm must have been of unusual intensity to have caused trained boatmen such fright. But even more amazing than that is the fact that in the midst of the storm they, who were trained, skilled boatmen, turn for help to one who was utterly devoid of any skill in such matters.

Already they have learned, however inarticulately, that this unusual man always proves to be the master of every situation. Now faced with fear of an unusual storm, they find themselves instinctively turning to him for help. They turn to one who in the midst of the storm was sleeping like a little child, to one who had no fear of anything earthly. His very words to them breathe the spirit of calm, " Why are ye full of fears? How is it that ye do not trust God? "

No sooner is their fear of the storm quieted than it is replaced by a new and very different kind of fear — a fear which is close to awe. "They feared exceedingly." The disciples are beginning to have more than ordinary human reactions to this man. Who is he? They do not know.

23 NAZARETH

And he went out from thence, and came into his own country; and his disciples follow him. And when the sabbath day was come, he began to teach in the synagogue: and many hearing him were astonished, saying, From whence hath this man these things? and what wisdom is this which is given unto him, that even such mighty works are wrought by his hands? Is not this the carpenter, the son of Mary, the brother of James, and Joses, and of Juda, and Simon? and are not his sisters here with us? And they were offended at him.

But Jesus said unto them, A prophet is not without honour, but in his own country, and among his own kin, and in his own house. And he could there do no mighty work, save that he laid his hands upon a few sick folk, and healed them. And he marvelled because of their unbelief. And he went round about the villages, teaching.

Mark 6: 1-6

It would seem probable that this event occurred sometime earlier in the Galilean ministry than where Mark places it. Already we know that Jesus is for all practical purposes excommunicate from the synagogues, with many of the Pharisees set solidly against him and his teaching. We presume therefore that this event took place fairly early in his ministry to the towns of Galilee, soon after the report of the mighty acts done at Capernaum had spread to Nazareth, and certainly before the visit of his family to Capernaum to bring him home, thinking him to be insane.

This passage is our only intimation that there were brothers and sisters in Jesus' family. The definite names of four brothers are given and it is stated that there were at least two sisters. The fact that Joseph is not here mentioned is sure evidence that he was no longer alive.

In Jesus' words at Nazareth we have his own disclosure that those of his own town and family did not believe in him. The spirit in Nazareth is pictured as hostile and critical. Jesus marvelled at their unbelief, i.e., their insensitivity and unresponsiveness to the presence and power of God in him to heal them.

24 THE DEATH OF JOHN THE BAPTIST

And King Herod heard of him; (for his name was spread abroad:) and he said, That John the Baptist was risen from the dead, and therefore mighty works do shew forth themselves in him. Others said, That it is Elias. And others said, That it is a prophet, or as one of the prophets. But when Herod heard thereof, he said, It is John, whom I beheaded: he is risen from the dead.

For Herod himself had sent forth and laid hold upon John, and bound him in prison for Herodias' sake, his brother Philip's wife: for he had married her. For John had said unto Herod, It is not lawful for thee to have thy brother's wife. Therefore Herodias had a quarrel against him, and would have killed him; but she could not: for Herod feared John, knowing that he was a just man and an holy, and observed him; and when he heard him, he did many things, and heard him gladly.

And when a convenient day was come, that Herod on his birthday made a supper to his lords, high captains, and chief estates of Galilee; and when the daughter of the said Herodias came in, and danced, . . . the king said unto the damsel, Ask of me whatsoever thou wilt, and I will give it thee. And he sware unto her, Whatsoever thou shalt ask of me, I will give it thee, unto the half of my kingdom.

And she went forth, and said unto her mother, What shall I ask? And she said, The head of John the Baptist. And she came in straightway with haste unto the king, and asked, saying, I will that thou give me by and by in a charger the head of John the Baptist.

And the king was exceeding sorry; yet for his oath's sake, and for their sakes which sat with him, he would not reject her. And immediately the king sent an executioner, and commanded his head to be brought: and he went and beheaded him in the prison, and brought his head in a charger, and gave it to the damsel: and the damsel gave it to her mother. And when his disciples heard of it, they came and took up his corpse, and laid it in a tomb.

Mark 6: 14-29

Jesus' ministry in its beginning synchronized very closely with that of John the Baptist. Jesus had undergone baptism at his hands. Immediately upon the arrest of John, he had begun his ministry in Galilee. Now the report brought to Jesus of the death of John was an omen to Jesus of his own coming fate. In order to think upon the significance of the death of John the Baptist, whom he (and he alone) knew to be the forerunner, Jesus desired to withdraw from Galilee and go again into the wilderness to be alone with God in prayer, and then to prepare the disciples for that which lay ahead.

This passage is of great significance in that it clearly informs us that neither King Herod nor the people of Galilee have the slightest suspicion that Jesus is or claims to be the Messiah of God. Rather they judge him to be a prophet, or at the highest, Elijah. According to Jewish tradition, Elijah had never died but instead had been translated into the heavenly world without going through death. Then there was the great prophecy concerning him in the book of the prophet Malachi — " Behold, I will send you Elijah the prophet before the coming of the great and dreadful day of the Lord." The popular term for the expected Elijah was " he that should come." The people of Galilee were then looking for the return of Elijah; only when he should have come would they then look for the Messiah. Jesus, although he had done many mighty works in the true pattern of Elijah, yet did not live as an ascetic. John the Baptist, on the contrary, lived the ascetic life such as Elijah had lived, but performed no miracles. Thus nobody, not even John himself, suspected that John was the " forerunner," " he that should come," the Elijah returned to earth. Jesus knew that John was the Elijah, because he knew himself to be the Messiah. We, who from our vantage point in history know John to have been the forerunner, must not believe that the people of Galilee so looked upon John and Jesus.

Jesus is determined now to leave Galilee. Already he had

visited most of the towns and villages of Galilee, proclaiming the advent of the kingdom of God and calling men to enter into that kingdom through repentance. Nothing would be gained by remaining longer in Galilee. With the premonition of coming death for himself, Jesus desired to take his disciples apart from the throngs and excitement of Galilee and to go into territory where he could get quiet and isolation, a period of retreat in which to be in the presence of God and learn of that which God willed for him.

But it will not be easy for him to withdraw from Galilee and the popular following which surrounded him. Thinking him to be perhaps the returned Elijah, the people would be loath to let him out of their sight, lest when the Messiah appeared they be not at hand.

PART THREE

WITHDRAWAL FROM GALILEE

25 A SUMMARY OF THE PERIOD

We shall notice a new tone in Jesus' teaching from this time forth, a note dealing with the cost of following him, the note of the Cross. Because of this new tone, a large majority of the people will turn back from following him. For a time it must have appeared likely that even some of the twelve would abandon Jesus, for the Gospel recorded by John informs us that one day Jesus asked them, " Will ye also go away? "

No period of Jesus' ministry is for us more confusing and bewildering than this period which we are about to study. We are confronted here in Mark with what seem to be two different traditions which are joined together in baffling form by Mark. They picture to us Jesus with his disciples as undertaking many meaningless crossings of the lake, and as yet never arriving at any destination. We have a second account of a miraculous feeding, as if a first one had never occurred at all. Moreover, we have a saying of Jesus which infers the passage of considerable time in or near the cities of Bethsaida and Chorazin; yet our gospel records tell us nothing of that ministry.

It will be helpful therefore if we seek to sketch an outline of what seems probably the itinerary of this next period. After leaving Capernaum in Peter's boat, with the purpose of going for rest and retirement into the sparsely inhabited region at the northeast portion of the lake, Jesus is met on the shore by a large following of Galileans, who are unwilling to let him leave Galilee. Jesus spends some days, even perhaps some weeks,

teaching them here; and in this teaching for the first time comes
.the note of warning of the Cross.

Then Jesus finally had a meal of very solemn nature with the
multitude, a meal which betokened to the crowd his promise
that when the Messianic banquet took place they would be
guests. Then Jesus sent the crowd away, and a short time later,
with three chosen disciples, withdrew to a nearby mountain
for the experience which we call the Transfiguration. There
for the first time the secret of his being the Messiah is revealed
to them by the voice of God, an announcement which they are
commanded by Jesus to keep secret.

Next, after a short visit back to Capernaum to return Peter's
boat, Jesus withdraws northward into the region belonging to
the cities of Tyre and Sidon, a period of time which may have
lasted as long as ten months, and on which we have but very
little data. Then we find them at Caesarea Philippi, where by
the impetuous action of Peter the secret of Jesus' messiahship
is made known to the twelve, and again they are sworn to
solemn secrecy. Jesus at once tells them of his forthcoming
death at Jerusalem, an event which they are utterly unable to
conceive or accept.

Then Jesus passes secretly through Galilee and journeys up
to Jerusalem to his death. It is in this last journey to Jerusalem
and the events that will happen there, that we acquire our
fullest knowledge of Jesus.

26 SEEKING RETREAT ACROSS THE LAKE

And the apostles gathered themselves together unto Jesus, and told
him all things, both what they had done, and what they had taught. And
he said unto them, Come ye yourselves apart in a desert place, and rest a
while: for there were many coming and going, and they had no leisure
so much as to eat. And they departed into a desert place by ship privately.
                                                            Mark 6: 30-32

As a sort of farewell gesture, Jesus had sent out his disciples
two by two on a tour of the towns and villages of Galilee, to

proclaim the nearness of the kingdom of God and to preach repentance. Apparently during their absence word was brought to Jesus of the death of John the Baptist.

Jesus feels a pressure from God to withdraw from Galilee. For him John's death is the signal that his own ministry is fast approaching its end, and he wants to retire from the crowds to be alone with God in prayer. Also he will need now to train and prepare his disciples for that which lies ahead.

Setting forth therefore in a small boat — presumably one belonging to Peter — Jesus bade his disciples sail eastward across the lake, hoping to disembark in the region east of Bethsaida, where there was much uninhabited territory.

27 IMPOSSIBILITY OF ESCAPE

And the people saw them departing, and many knew him, and ran afoot thither out of all cities, and outwent them, and came together unto him.

And Jesus, when he came out, saw much people, and was moved with compassion toward them, because they were as sheep not having a shepherd: and he began to teach them many things.

Mark 6: 33-34

The Galilean crowds were unwilling that Jesus should leave them. Was he not their Elijah? By keeping close to him, would they not then be assured that when the Messiah came, they would be on hand to enter into the blessings of the new, Messianic Age?

From the shore at Capernaum they would quickly be able to determine to what point on the opposite shore of the lake Jesus and his disciples were headed. Then, by the simple procedure of walking along the shore, they were enabled to outdistance the boat and be on the beach waiting when Jesus disembarked. What Jesus found was not quiet and solitude, but an eager, excited crowd.

To Jesus they appeared as sheep lost and wandering, with no wise and loving shepherd to lead them. Taking compassion upon them, Jesus proceeded to teach them — we presume about the coming of the kingdom of God. It may well have been that some weeks were spent in the vicinity of Bethsaida, teaching the crowds. Portions of what we call the Sermon on the Mount may well have been given by Jesus in his teaching at this time. For much of the teaching of Jesus given us in the Gospels we have neither chronology nor setting. We are thus left with the problem of assigning the material to different periods of his ministry as best we may.

28 A SACRED MEAL

When the day was now far spent, his disciples came unto him, and said, This is a desert place, and now the time is far passed: send them away, that they may go into the country round about, and into the villages, and buy themselves bread: for they have nothing to eat. He answered and said unto them, Give ye them to eat. And they say unto him, Shall we go and buy two hundred pennyworth of bread, and give them to eat? He saith unto them, How many loaves have ye? go and see. And when they knew, they say, Five, and two fishes.

And he commanded them to make all sit down by companies upon the green grass. And they sat down in ranks, by hundreds, and by fifties. And when he had taken the five loaves and the two fishes, he looked up to heaven, and blessed, and brake the loaves, and gave them to his disciples to set before them; and the two fishes divided he among them all. And they did all eat, and were filled. . . . And they that did eat of the loaves were about five thousand men.

Mark 6: 35-42, 44

On one of the days when Jesus was teaching the crowds near Bethsaida, the people were unwilling to leave Jesus, even though the day was drawing near to its close. They sensed somehow that mighty things were about to happen. Believing that Jesus might be their Elijah, they hung expectantly about him, as if at any moment the Messiah might appear.

Jesus answered their mood with a great event — a solemn, sacred meal in which he was host and the whole multitude his guests. Jesus received from his band of disciples five loaves and two fishes — that which would be the daily food of Galilean

peasants. There is no situation of a starving crowd. They had only to go into the nearby towns and villages to secure sufficient food for their needs. This meal is not a hunger-satisfying meal, but rather a sacred, sacramental meal.

Mark has described the situation simply. Jesus bade the people sit down by companies of fifties and hundreds. Finally only Jesus remained standing in their midst. A hush pervaded the whole scene. Jesus, with every eye fastened upon him, took into his hands the bread and the fishes, looked up to heaven, said a blessing, broke the loaves, and then gave the parts to his disciples to distribute to the multitude, seated on the grass.

As simple as that. Yet both for Jesus and for the crowd the event was filled with a solemn, sacred significance. Closely associated with the expectation of the coming of the Messiah was the hope of being a guest at a great Messianic banquet, inaugurating the coming of the new Messianic Age. For the crowd, here was their Elijah, giving them a foretaste of that great Messianic banquet, a solemn pledge that when that day came they would be with him. For Jesus, knowing himself to be not the Elijah, but the Messiah, the deed meant much more than that. It expressed for him his deep desire to give his life to each and all of these folk, who were like sheep without a shepherd. It was also for him a farewell banquet for his people.

"They did all eat, and were filled." What does the word "filled" refer to? Their stomachs? Or are we to give a much deeper, spiritual significance to that word, such as we commonly do when we receive in the Holy Communion a fragment of bread and a few drops of wine, and know that we are filled with the indwelling of the risen Jesus?

We must recognize frankly that it is in only one verse, the 43d, that there is even a hint of a material miracle. There is, of course, no possible way for us to be sure of the text that Mark originally wrote or to get back through the earlier oral tradition to the actual historical event. By the time that we

have our earliest quotations and manuscript evidence, there is ample time for many editors to have worked over the story. Did some well-intentioned Christian scribe, reading the original words " and they were all filled " then proceed to amplify it by adding that one sentence, " and they took up twelve baskets full of the fragments, and of the fishes " ? Intending to heighten the wonder of the event, he has instead changed a spiritual event into a crude, physical miracle without meaning. We cannot but remember Jesus' rejection in the wilderness of the way of miracle to bring men into the Kingdom.

There is still further inferential evidence which supports this interpretation of this event. Had there been the actual multiplication of the loaves and fishes, we should certainly have expected in our account some note of unparalleled excitement as the sequel. There is none such in the three earliest gospel accounts. Only in the late tradition of John do we have that which we would then expect — an attempt to force Jesus to be their Messiah then and there. Yet we know that nobody even suspected that Jesus was more than Elijah.

Instead of that sequel, we find Jesus calmly sending his disciples away by boat to Bethsaida, and then the crowds also. The whole mood of this event, as it is described for us by Mark, is one of calm and peace, and of solemn, sacred mystery.

Moreover, shortly after this event, both Mark and Matthew record these words of Jesus addressed to Pharisees, who came seeking from him a sign from heaven, "An evil and adulterous generation seeketh after a sign; and there shall no sign [miracle] be given to it, but the sign of the prophet Jonas [Jonah]." And we greatly err when we think of the sign of Jonah as being his living for three days within the whale. The sign of Jonah is *repentance.* That sign is a spiritual sign, and it is the only sign that Jesus would give to his generation. It is very difficult to believe that Jesus uttered these words to the Pharisees if only a short time before he had performed this stupendous, material miracle.

A widespread interpretation of this event on the lines that a young lad, unselfishly bringing forth his own meager food supply, inspired everybody else to pool his own supply of food, entirely misses the point which is all-important, i.e., that it is Jesus, and not the crowd, who is host. Such an interpretation robs Jesus of his unique role of being the sole host with everybody else his guests.

Unquestionably then we interpret this meal as a sacred, sacramental meal, embodying Jesus' last farewell to the Galileans, a token of the coming Messianic banquet which would be held in heaven, and at which again Jesus would be host as God's Messiah.

29 JESUS ON THE BEACH

Straightway he constrained his disciples to get into the ship, and to go to the other side before unto Bethsaida, while he sent away the people. And when he had sent them away, he departed into a mountain to pray.

And when even was come, the ship was in the midst of the sea, and he alone on the land. And he saw them toiling in rowing; for the wind was contrary unto them: and about the fourth watch of the night . . . they see Jesus walking on the sea, and drawing nigh unto the ship: and they were afraid. But he saith unto them, It is I; be not afraid. Then they willingly received him into the ship: and immediately the ship was at the land whither they went.

Mark 6: 45-48a and John 6: 19b-21

The disciples of Jesus had only to skirt the shore of the lake and they would quickly have found themselves back at Bethsaida. But they had been deeply moved by the sacred meal, not understanding however what it meant. So deeply stirred were they by it all that they awoke to find themselves out in the middle of the lake, rowing against a strong head wind. For the rest of the night they toiled against the wind and waves, and only close to dawn did they finally draw near to the shore, there to behold Jesus, whom they had left across the lake. They thought they were seeing a ghost, and more than that, a ghost walking upon the water.

Many years ago a friend and myself were making a canoe trip on Lake George in New York State. One day we found ourselves caught in a heavy offshore wind. The person whose home we were headed for was standing on the low shore waiting for us, as we paddled against the wind and waves. With the crests of the waves in the line of our vision, and with the low beach shut off from our sight by the high waves, it actually looked as if he were walking upon the waves, as he walked to and fro on the beach. May it not have been something like that which lies behind our record of this event on the Lake of Galilee? John's record of the event states " and immediately the ship was at the land whither they went." Jesus had only to walk along the shore from the place where the meal had been held to outstrip the disciples rowing throughout the night.

30 THE FIRST PREACHING OF THE CROSS

And when he had called the people unto him with his disciples also, he said unto them, Whosoever will come after me, let him deny himself, and take up his cross, and follow me. For whosoever will save his life shall lose it; but whosoever shall lose his life for my sake and the gospel's, the same shall save it. For what shall it profit a man, if he shall gain the whole world, and lose his own soul? Or what shall a man give in exchange for his soul? Whosoever therefore shall be ashamed of me and of my words in this adulterous and sinful generation; of him also shall the Son of Man be ashamed, when he cometh in the glory of his Father with the holy angels.

And he said unto them, Verily I say unto you, That there be some of them that stand here, which shall not taste of death, till they have seen the kingdom of God come with power.

Mark 8: 34-38; 9: 1

Here we are given by Mark a sample of the sort of teaching which Jesus gave at this time to the crowds of people in or near Bethsaida. We unmistakably discern in the teaching the new note of danger and of the Cross.

In this particular teaching Jesus uses an astounding comparison. On one side he places the whole world; on the other side of the balance one single life, lost or saved. The imagery recalls to our minds the satanic temptation, in which Satan showed to Jesus all the kingdoms of the world in a moment of time, with the promise that all should be his if he would but worship Satan.

Jesus here carefully refers to the Son of Man, another popular term for the Messiah, in the third person, thus safeguarding his own Messianic secret. All that he hints openly here is that there exists a close identification of himself with the one to be at last accepted as the coming Messiah. We also have the disclosure by Jesus himself that the Kingdom will come in the lifetime of his own generation.

31 THE PHARISEES SEEK AFTER A SIGN

The Pharisees came forth, and began to question with him, seeking of him a sign from heaven, tempting him. And he sighed deeply in his spirit, and saith,

An evil and adulterous generation seeketh after a sign; and there shall no sign be given to it, but the sign of the prophet Jonas. . . . The men of Nineveh shall rise in judgment with this generation, and shall condemn it: because they repented at the preaching of Jonas; and, behold, a greater than Jonas is here.

Mark 8: 11-12a and Matthew 12: 39b, 41

Again we find Jesus confronted with the critical and hostile Pharisees, seeking to trap him. We remember that already there is a plot being fomented to bring about the death of Jesus on the part of the Pharisees and Herodians.

This passage has about it the ring of authenticity. It fits in perfectly with the temptation stories. The Pharisees' question is nothing more than the satanic temptation to prove his authority by astounding men with a miracle. Long ago Jesus had accepted the fact that the kingdom of God can never come by the way of miracles, but only by the way appointed by God — repentance. Jesus remains faithful to the way chosen of God.

32 WOE TO THREE GALILEAN TOWNS

Then began he to upbraid the cities wherein most of his mighty works were done, because they repented not: Woe unto thee, Chorazin! woe unto thee, Bethsaida! for if the mighty works, which were done in you, had been done in Tyre and Sidon, they would have repented long ago in sackcloth and ashes. But I say unto you, It shall be more tolerable for Tyre and Sidon at the day of judgment, than for you.

And thou, Capernaum, which art exalted unto heaven, shalt be brought down to hell: for if the mighty works, which have been done in thee, had been done in Sodom, it would have remained until this day. But I say unto you, That it shall be more tolerable for the land of Sodom in the day of judgment, than for thee.

Matthew 11: 20-24

This passage hints at an important and apparently more than temporary ministry of Jesus in three important Galilean cities — Capernaum, Chorazin, and Bethsaida. Our gospel records give us only a few scattered pictures of the Capernaum ministry and almost nothing of the ministry in the other two regions.

Again we have the note of repentance stressed as the keynote. Jesus judges these three cities alike. They would not repent. They had heard the good news from God and would not respond to it. There remained now for the three cities the judgment of God in the last great day.

33 COMMANDMENTS OF GOD AND TRADITIONS OF MEN

Then came together unto him the Pharisees, and certain of the scribes, which came from Jerusalem. And when they saw some of his disciples eat bread with defiled, that is to say, with unwashen, hands, they found fault. For the Pharisees, and all the Jews, except they wash their hands oft, eat not, holding the tradition of the elders. And when they come from the market, except they wash, they eat not. And many other things there be, which they have received to hold, as the washing of cups, and pots, brasen vessels, and of tables.

Then the Pharisees and scribes asked him, Why walk not thy disciples according to the tradition of the elders, but eat bread with unwashen hands? He answered and said unto them, Well hath Isaiah prophesied of you hypocrites, as it is written, This people honoureth me with their lips, but their heart is far from me. Howbeit in vain do they worship me, teaching for doctrines the commandments of men. For laying aside the commandment of God, ye hold the tradition of men, as the washing of pots and cups: and many other such like things ye do.

And he said unto them, Full well ye reject the commandment of God, that ye may keep your own tradition. For Moses said, Honour thy father and thy mother; and, Whoso curseth father or mother, let him die the death: But ye say, If a man shall say to his father or mother, It is Corban, that is to say, a gift, by whatsoever thou mightest be profited by me; he shall be free. And ye suffer him no more to do ought for his father or his mother; making the word of God of none effect through your tradition, which ye have delivered: and many such like things do ye.

And when he had called all the people unto him, he said unto them, Hearken unto me every one of you, and understand: There is nothing from without a man, that entering into him can defile him: but the things which come out of him, those are they that defile the man. . . . For from within, out of the heart of men, proceed evil thoughts, adulteries, fornications, murders, thefts, covetousness, wickedness, deceit, lasciviousness, an evil eye, blasphemy, pride, foolishness: all these evil things come from within, and defile the man. . . . If any man have ears to hear, let him hear.

Mark 7: 1-15, 21-23, 16

This is the final conflict which Mark records for us in this period of the Galilean ministry. Jesus is about to leave Galilee for the region of Tyre and Sidon. In this conflict Jesus is by no means conciliatory. He in no way fears his powerful adversaries, not even those which have come down from Jerusalem — ominous though that fact be. We can picture the scorn of these superior Jerusalem scribes for Jesus and for his simple Galilean disciples, as they observed how they ate food with unwashed hands. We can smile at the meticulous and ridiculous care of these religious experts for non-essentials.

Jesus pours forth his scorn for their hypocrisy. " Well hath Isaiah prophesied of you hypocrites. For *laying aside the commandment of God*, ye hold the tradition of men." Always religion is fraught with this danger of man-made rules and traditions, pushing aside the true commandments of God. There were only ten commandments from God. But the religious leaders of the ages had added hundreds of others to those ten, until there were now so many that it was almost impossible not to break one of them daily.

Jesus does not deal with generalities. He will give them a definite example. God had given a commandment which involved the care of father and mother in their old age by their own children. But the Pharisees had cleverly managed to circumvent that law by a tradition of men, under which a man could deed his property or wealth to God, while still retaining a life use of it himself, and by that subterfuge be unable to care for his aged parents. Such procedure is to make the traditions of men count more than the commandments of God.

Then Jesus proceeds to give his own keen diagnosis of that which lies deep in the hearts of men. His list is substantiated by the experience of any psychiatrist today. Each of us knows that we dare not challenge the truth of Jesus' diagnosis. Not very likely material upon which to build a kingdom of God! But Jesus did not build the Kingdom upon men, good or righteous. He knew that the Kingdom was built, not by men, but by God.

34 TRANSFIGURATION

It came to pass about an eight days after these sayings, he took Peter and John and James, and went up into a mountain to pray. And as he prayed, the fashion of his countenance was altered, and his raiment was white and glistering. And, behold, there talked with him two men, which were Moses and Elias: who appeared in glory, and spake of his decease which he should accomplish at Jerusalem.

But Peter and they that were with him were heavy with sleep: and when they were awake, they saw his glory, and the two men that stood with him. And it came to pass, as they departed from him, Peter said unto Jesus, Master, it is good for us to be here: and let us make three tabernacles; one for thee, and one for Moses, and one for Elias: not knowing what he said.

While he thus spake, there came a cloud, and overshadowed them: and they feared as they entered into the cloud. And there came a voice out of the cloud, saying, This is my beloved Son: hear him. And when the voice was past, Jesus was found alone. . . .

And as they came down from the mountain, he charged them that they should tell no man what things they had seen, till the Son of Man were risen from the dead. And they kept that saying with themselves, questioning one with another what the rising from the dead should mean.

And they asked him, saying, Why say the scribes that Elias must first come? And he answered and told them, Elias verily cometh first, and restoreth all things; and how it is written of the Son of Man, that he must suffer many things, and be set at nought. But I say unto you, That Elias is indeed come, and they have done unto him whatsoever they listed, as it is written of him.

Luke 9: 28-36a and Mark 9: 9-13

The story of the Transfiguration, placed as it is in our Gospels after the confession of Peter at Caesarea Philippi, loses most of its deep and rich significance. If Peter and the other disciples already know that Jesus is the Messiah, we can see little meaning to the journey up the mountain and to the events which take place there. In the account of Caesarea Philippi as related by Matthew, Peter's confession is answered by Jesus with these words, " Blessed art thou, Simon Bar-jona: for flesh and blood hath not revealed it unto thee, but my Father which is in heaven." It is thus definitely stated that Peter's confession of Jesus being the Messiah was due, not to Peter's exceptional insight, but to some event in which it was revealed to him by God. Yet, nowhere else in the gospel accounts are we given the story of that revelation by God to Peter, unless it be here in the events of the Transfiguration experience. When this event is placed at the close of the ministry at Bethsaida, and some nine or ten months preceding the confession of Peter at Caesarea Philippi, then both of the events take on a much richer and deeper significance.

With this perspective let us now turn to the story. Jesus had left Capernaum, intending to find solitude for himself and for his disciples in the region near the northeast part of the Lake of Galilee. Arriving there, he finds that the crowds from Capernaum have followed him by way of the shore, and Jesus then spends perhaps some weeks in or near Bethsaida, teaching the people. Eight days after these sayings — and since we do not have anything like a full account of these days of teaching, we cannot know to what the " eight days after these sayings " refers — Jesus took with him Peter, and John, and James and went up into a mountain to pray. Here again we are given one of the very few references to Jesus at prayer; and we rightly expect that something momentous is about to happen. We presume that the mountain of the Transfiguration is one of the low mountains near by Bethsaida, east of the lake. We must remember that none of the disciples even suspect that Jesus is the Messiah of God. That he is a very unusual man they do know.

It is apparently nighttime, for we find the disciples heavy with sleep. Perhaps there was a full moon, and the mountain top where they were would be bathed in the silvery light of the moon. While the three disciples slept, Jesus had an experience which he has described for us in terms of a vision and of a communion with two persons from the other world, Moses and Elijah. For a few moments the veil which separates that world from this was lifted, and Jesus, Moses, and Elijah conversed together concerning the death that he is to suffer at Jerusalem. The ministry upon earth of Jesus is not simply his own concern, but that of the heavenly world also. Jesus had so rich and living a fellowship with them that he can describe it to us in terms of a vision in which he talks with them, and they with him.

For Jesus the Transfiguration is the clear confirmation of that which had been hinted at in the wilderness temptations, when there had come to Jesus the first intimation that the end of his ministry might be rejection and death. From this moment on Jesus accepts, as appointed for him by God, the cross of death. Not by his proclaiming of the coming of the Kingdom will it come. People will not be called to repentance by his preaching or his mighty works. In the inscrutable strategy of God the way of death is the appointed way in which the Kingdom is to come. All the more now Jesus needs solitude and quiet, both to prepare himself for his coming death, some ten months later in Jerusalem, and to prepare his disciples for their acceptance of death for him. Truly, in Jesus' life the Transfiguration stands out as one of the climactic points of his ministry. It was there on the mountain top that Jesus accepted from afar the crucifixion.

The Transfiguration is also a high-water mark in the ministry of Jesus for the disciples. Here, for the first time, and then not as a perception based upon their own insight, but as a revelation given by God, the three disciples learn that Jesus is the Son of Man, the Messiah of God. Peter's impulsive words, " Master, it is good for us to be here," are at once corrected by a voice from heaven, " This is my beloved Son: hear him." This is the second time that this key word is used. We met with it first in the baptismal experience, where again it was a word spoken by a heavenly voice. " This is no human Rabbi, Master, Teacher. This is my *unique* Son." From this time forth the disciples will stand in awe of Jesus — this being who is truly human and yet also the chosen Messiah of God, and the king of the coming Messianic Kingdom. The tremendous secret of Jesus is no longer his secret alone. Peter, John, and James now share it. So, far from being a meaningless incident, we perceive that the Transfiguration is of the greatest importance in the understanding of the whole ministry of Jesus.

The three disciples are now confronted with a new and puzzling idea. Coming down from the mountain, Jesus charged them to keep secret the revelation which had been given them " until the Son of Man were risen from the dead." The two terms — " Son of Man " and " death " — simply do not, in their minds, go together. We remember that there was nothing in Jewish expectations for the Messiah which could hold any place for death. This new conception was as inconceivable as to believe that God could die. Their minds were wholly unable to accept this new idea.

They are then confronted with still another puzzle. Everybody had been looking for Elijah, as the one who would prepare the way for the coming of the Messiah. Now they had just learned that Jesus was the Messiah. But where then was Elijah? Why had he not first come? Proof conclusive that none of them conceived John the Baptist to have been Elijah. It is only now when Jesus hints that Elijah has come and gone that they waken to the fact that their timetable is all wrong.

35 HEALING

When he came to his disciples, he saw a great multitude about them, and the scribes questioning with them. And straightway all the people, when they beheld him, were greatly amazed, and running to him saluted him. And he asked the scribes, What question ye with them?

And one of the multitude answered and said, Master, I have brought unto thee my son, which hath a dumb spirit; and wheresoever he taketh him, he teareth him: and he foameth, and gnasheth with his teeth, and pineth away: and I spake to thy disciples that they should cast him out; and they could not. He answereth him and saith, O faithless generation, how long shall I be with you? how long shall I suffer you? bring him unto me.

And they brought him unto him: and when he saw him, straightway the spirit tare him; and he fell on the ground, and wallowed foaming. And he asked his father, How long is it ago since this came unto him? And he said, Of a child. And ofttimes it hath cast him into the fire, and into the waters, to destroy him: but if thou canst do any thing, have compassion on us, and help us.

Jesus said unto him, If thou canst believe, all things are possible to him that believeth. And straightway the father of the child cried out, and said with tears, Lord, I believe; help thou mine unbelief. When Jesus saw that the people came running together, he rebuked the foul spirit, saying unto him, Thou dumb and deaf spirit, I charge thee, come out of him, and enter no more into him. And the spirit cried, and rent him sore, and came out of him: and he was as one dead; insomuch that many said, He is dead. But Jesus took him by the hand, and lifted him up; and he arose.

And when he was come into the house, his disciples asked him privately, Why could not we cast him out? And he said unto them, This kind can come forth by nothing, but by prayer.

Mark 9: 14-29

Here again we have supplemental confirmation of our belief that the Transfiguration took place, not in pagan territory near Caesarea Philippi, but in the region near Bethsaida. Only so can we account for the crowds which at once run to Jesus as he comes down from the mountain of the Transfiguration. Here near Bethsaida we find the crowds of Galilean people; in pagan territory we would not expect such a crowd.

As we are already familiar with the healing power of Jesus, we need not give detailed attention to this particular incident. But we do need to give attention to the question which the disciples ask Jesus, and to the reply that Jesus makes. " Why could not *we* cast him out? " Dare we to assume that the disciples had presumed to cast out the devil, without due dependence upon God, seeking to do the exorcism in their own name? So easily powers, entrusted to us by God, become subtly transformed into self-contained talents, and we seek to exercise those powers in our own rights. And is there a rebuke, however courteously given, in Jesus' reply, " This kind can come forth by nothing, but by prayer"? On the mountain Jesus had prayed, and out of that there had been given to Jesus the power of God to use now for the healing of this dumb and deaf man. Jesus cast out devils with the " finger of God," not in his own name.

PART FOUR

PERIOD OF WANDERING

36 THE SYROPHENICIAN WOMAN

From thence he arose, and went into the borders of Tyre and Sidon, and entered into an house, and would have no man know it: but he could not be hid. For a certain woman, whose young daughter had an unclean spirit, heard of him, and came and fell at his feet. The woman was a Greek, a Syrophenician by nation; and she besought him that he would cast forth the devil out of her daughter. But Jesus said unto her, Let the children first be filled: for it is not meet to take the children's bread, and to cast it unto the dogs. And she answered and said unto him, Yes, Lord: yet the dogs under the table eat of the children's crumbs. And he saith unto her, For this saying go thy way; the devil is gone out of thy daughter. And when she was come to her house, she found the devil gone out, and her daughter laid upon the bed.

Mark 7: 24-30

The names Tyre and Sidon refer not only to the cities on the Mediterranean coast, but also to that extensive region inland, north of Galilee. This region was predominantly pagan, and here Jesus could expect to get free from the Jewish crowds which thronged around him in Galilee. Into this region Jesus came with his disciples to get solitude and freedom. He may have remained in this territory for a period as long as ten months. Of no part of his ministry do we possess such meager history. We have been given only this one story of this whole period.

We can understand Jesus' reluctance to cast forth the devil from the young daughter of the Syrophenician woman. He had come to this territory to escape the crowds and public acclaim, so that he might quietly and in secret prepare himself and his disciples for the end – his death. Let him perform but one miracle and at once he would again be besieged by people eager for cures.

But the woman had faith and determination, gifts from God, and she exercised those gifts to the full. Her need was unselfish and desperate. She asked not for herself, but for her daughter. Jesus would develop her faith even further. Would her faith be strong enough to overcome obstacles? Could she stand rebuke and scorn? "It is not meet to take the children's bread and to cast it unto the dogs." Even that could not break the woman's desire and hope. She was willing to be counted a dog, if only she might eat of the crumbs which fell from the children's meal. The will of God in Jesus to bestow healing meets with the faith in the woman, given by God and exercised by her. Jesus heals her daughter, and that by a word at a distance.

Here again we have an insight into the amazing faith of Jesus in God. With no hesitation, Jesus commands the healing of the girl and expects that God will immediately accomplish it. Jesus knows that he speaks the words of God with authority. What is the nature of this close relationship between Jesus and God that enables him so to speak and command?

37 HEALING A DUMB MAN

And again, departing from the coasts of Tyre and Sidon, he came unto the sea of Galilee, through the midst of the coasts of Decapolis.

And they bring unto him one that was deaf, and had an impediment in his speech; and they beseech him to put his hand upon him. And he took him aside from the multitude, and put his fingers into his ears, and he spit, and touched his tongue; and looking up to heaven, he sighed, and saith unto him, Ephphatha, that is, Be opened.

And straightway his ears were opened, and the string of his tongue was loosed, and he spake plain.

And he charged them that they should tell no man: but the more he charged them, so much the more a great deal they published it; and were beyond measure astonished, saying, He hath done all things well: he maketh both the deaf to hear, and the dumb to speak.

Mark 7: 31-37

Perhaps some nine months after the preceding event, we find Jesus coming out of the pagan territory and again entering Galilee. We are therefore not surprised to find him at once surrounded by crowds. But Jesus, although from compassion he heals the sick man, is not yet ready to enter upon another public ministry in Galilee. Before beginning the journey up to Jerusalem, there is a momentous disclosure that needs to be made to all the disciples. Turning, therefore, again from Galilee and the crowds, he traveled northward to the region of Caesarea Philippi.

38 CAESAREA PHILIPPI

Jesus went out, and his disciples, into the towns of Caesarea Philippi: and by the way he asked his disciples, saying unto them, Whom do men say that I am? And they answered, John the Baptist: but some say, Elias; and others, One of the prophets. And he saith unto them, But whom say ye that I am? And Peter answereth and saith unto him, Thou art the Messiah.

And Jesus answered and said unto him, Blessed art thou, Simon Bar-jona: for flesh and blood hath not revealed it unto thee, but my Father which is in heaven. . . .

Then charged he his disciples that they should tell no man that he was Jesus the Messiah.

Mark 8: 27-29 and Matthew 16: 17, 20

This event is one of the climactic points in the whole ministry of Jesus. Placed as it is in our English Bibles as happening before the Transfiguration, it leaves us with problems that cannot be solved; but placed here, some nine or ten months after the Transfiguration, it fits in perfectly. Up to now only the three chosen disciples know that Jesus is the Messiah, a secret revealed to them in the Transfiguration. That secret they have kept over these many months. Presumably they have continued to be puzzled at Jesus' prediction that the Messiah must die and rise again.

Jesus is now about to go up to Jerusalem to die. The time has come when the disciples must be led to a decision as to who Jesus is. For a considerable time they have now followed Jesus. They have witnessed his mighty deeds. They have heard his teaching. They have been in closest fellowship with Jesus. What do they think concerning him? Jesus leads to the question he would ask them by asking first, " Whom do men say that I am? " To that question they can at once give an answer. Men think Jesus to be either Elijah or a prophet. Here again is clear indication that nobody in Galilee even suspects that Jesus is the Messiah. Then Jesus asks them, " But whom say *ye* that I am? After these many months of living with me, whom do you judge me to be? " Were they able to discern in him the very life and work of God?

Peter's impetuous reply forestalls whatever answer the disciples themselves might have been able to give. We are thus at a loss to know whether or not any of them had even begun to discern the true nature of Jesus, through his work, teaching, and life. Peter blurts out, " Thou art the Messiah."

We can picture in our imaginations the wide-opened mouths and eyes of the nine disciples. Jesus — the Messiah? How could that be? Did their minds, all too human, at once fill in the meaning of the term " Messiah " with their own preconceptions of what it must be? Jesus, who had chosen them, was to be the king of Israel. What would that mean for *them?* What would *they* have? But how had Peter found out this secret? Were there glances of jealousy directed towards him?

Matthew, in his account of this event, then records words, upon the basis of which we are led to pre-date the Transfiguration into the time of the Bethsaida ministry. Jesus states that Peter's confession is due not to any peculiar insight of his own, but rather to a revelation from God. "For flesh and blood hath not revealed it unto thee, but my Father which is in heaven." Those words, as we have already seen, must refer to the Transfiguration. Our belief in the messiahship of Jesus rests upon very wobbly foundations, if it rests simply upon the impetuous insight of Peter; but if it is rooted firmly in a revelation from God, then we need have no fear that it may be an erroneous idea. The disciples witnessed to the confession in the early church; but they knew that it did not originate with them. It was given to them. For what human mind could ever have conceived of God incarnate in a human man?

The secret of Jesus' being is now known to twelve — and only twelve — men, his chosen disciples. They at once are charged to keep it secret. They are to tell no man that he is the Messiah. We shall need to remember this solemn charge when we come to interpret the betrayal by Judas.

39 SATANIC TEMPTATION

And he began to teach them, that the Son of Man must suffer many things, and be rejected of the elders, and of the chief priests, and scribes, and be killed, and after three days rise again. And he spake that saying openly.

Then Peter took him, and began to rebuke him, saying, Be it far from thee, Messiah: this shall not be unto thee.

But when he had turned about and looked on his disciples, he rebuked Peter, saying, Get thee behind me, Satan: for thou savourest not the things that be of God, but the things that be of men.

Mark 8: 31-32a, 33 and Matthew 16: 22

Just as after the Transfiguration the disclosure of Jesus' messiahship to the three was at once followed by the puzzling and inconceivable prophecy by Jesus of his death and resurrection, so here we find the same thing occurring. No sooner have the nine learned that Jesus is the Messiah than they are startled and puzzled by his instant revelation to them of his coming death and resurrection.

We dare not explain away this basic record of our gospel traditions. We are in no way compelled by facts or reason to believe that only after the events did the disciples read back into the earthly ministry of Jesus this prediction. Our records have here the ring of stark, naked truth. They record both the prediction and the utter inability of the disciples to understand or accept it. We can well understand why that should have been so. There was no place in their reckonings for a suffering or a crucified Messiah. Accepting the fact that Jesus was the Messiah, they rejected as meaningless and impossible his death. We require just this psychological reaction in order to appreciate the shock and despair which will possess the disciples when Jesus is arrested in Gethsemane. Not once, but repeatedly, Jesus foretells the coming events; and the disciples reject his teachings as utterly impossible.

Peter, in his reaction to Jesus' prediction of his approaching death — " Be it far from thee, Messiah; this shall not be unto thee " — is not called " Blessed," but *Satan*. Just as Satan in the wilderness could disguise himself in the words of Scripture, so now he speaks through the closest of Jesus' disciples. Peter's thoughts and words are the thoughts and words of Satan. This is nothing more than a new form of the old temptation in the wilderness — " If thou be the Son of God . . . then no injury can happen unto thee."

But Jesus had received from God, and had obediently accepted, the vocation of the Cross. And here was a loved and trusted disciple tempting him to abandon the way appointed by God for a way appointed by Satan. For ten long months Jesus had been undergoing the agony of preparing for the Cross at Jerusalem, and now, with but two weeks lying ahead, Peter was seeking to divert him. Here, as had happened in the wilderness temptations, Jesus obeys God, not Satan. Not for one moment does Jesus dally with the tempting plan of Satan — that it is possible to be God's Messiah in some other way than that of the Cross. Who is this Jesus who so steadfastly has already begun to walk the way of the Cross?

40 PROPHECY OF DEATH AND RESURRECTION

They departed thence, and passed through Galilee; and he would not that any man should know it. For he taught his disciples, and said unto them, The Son of Man is delivered into the hands of men, and they shall kill him; and after that he is killed, he shall rise the third day. But they understood not that saying, and were afraid to ask him.

Mark 9: 30-32

This is the transition passage from one part of Jesus' ministry to another — the last. Not more than two weeks are required in which to place all the events of the last period of his ministry which the gospel writers record. The Galilean ministry may have been as short as a few months in duration. That would have been ample to have contained all that we know of his ministry there. The sojourn in the territory of Tyre and Sidon, which may have taken as much as ten months, gives us only a few incidents in our Gospels. But this last period, which may be as short as two weeks, takes the major portion of each of the Gospels. Here we know with much deeper certainty the chronology of events. It is into this decisive period that we now enter.

PART FIVE

JOURNEY TO JERUSALEM

41 GREATNESS

He came to Capernaum: and being in the house he asked them, What was it that ye disputed among yourselves by the way? But they held their peace: for by the way they had disputed among themselves, who should be the greatest. And he sat down, and called the twelve, and saith unto them, If any man desire to be first, the same shall be last of all, and servant of all. And he took a child, and set him in the midst of them: and when he had taken him in his arms, he said unto them, Whosoever shall receive one of such children in my name, receiveth me: and whosoever shall receive me, receiveth not me, but him that sent me.

Mark 9: 33-37

We picture Jesus and his disciples arriving quietly and secretly in Capernaum, perhaps late in the evening, and lodging in the home of Peter. It even may have been that the dispute which they had begun on the road, and which, although they were walking a little distance behind Jesus, he had overheard, was still continuing in Peter's home. Jesus quietly bids them to gather around him, and then seating himself, as a teacher, he teaches them a deep lesson in greatness.

Perhaps the background for the dispute lay in the fact that the nine disciples were jealous of Peter, James, and John, who had known of the Messianic secret months before them. Would Peter, James, and John also succeed in securing the foremost places in the coming Messianic kingdom, which they took for granted would be an earthly, economic-political kingdom? What positions would fall to each of them in that kingdom? We can picture them imagining themselves in positions of high authority. The only difficulty would be that of getting, each of them, a promise of high position from Jesus.

Jesus asks them a question, " What was it that ye disputed among yourselves by the way? " It was not that they could not tell him; rather it was that they felt shame before him. They had caught enough of his spirit to know that only by a subterfuge could they possibly secure his favor. So little did they know Jesus. Jesus himself reveals to them, to their shame, that he had perceived and understood that of which they had disputed on the road.

Taking a little child — perhaps one of Peter's children — Jesus held him in his arms and taught them both by word and by deed. He is truly great, according to Jesus, who is the lowliest and can serve others the most. The measure of greatness lies not in lording it over others, but in serving others. To serve a little child, Jesus teaches, is to serve him; and to serve Jesus is to serve God. Jesus knew that his work on earth was not simply his own work, but the work done by God in and through him, so close was the identification of his life with God's. He, the Son of God, lovingly and joyfully stooped to the lowliest of roles — that of a servant — but these his disciples were seeking to ascend that they might be able to compel others to serve them. We marvel at the patient love and teaching of Jesus.

42 DIVORCE

He arose from thence, and cometh into the coasts of Judea by the farther side of Jordan: and the people resort unto him again; and, as he was wont, he taught them again.

And the Pharisees came to him, and asked him, Is it lawful for a man to put away his wife? tempting him. And he answered and said unto them, What did Moses command you? And they said, Moses suffered to write a bill of divorcement, and to put her away. And Jesus answered and said unto them, For the hardness of your heart he wrote you this precept. But from the beginning of the creation God made them male and female. For this cause shall a man leave his father and mother, and cleave to his wife; and they twain shall be one flesh: so then they are no more twain, but one flesh. What therefore God hath joined together, let not man put asunder.

And in the house his disciples asked him again of the same matter.

And he saith unto them, Whosoever shall put away his wife, and marry another, committeth adultery against her. And if a woman shall leave her husband, and be married to another, she committeth adultery.

Mark 10: 1-12

Jesus with his disciples has taken the pilgrim road from Galilee to Jerusalem, crossing the Jordan just south of the lower part of the Lake of Galilee so as to journey through Judean territory and not through the land of the Samaritans. We are not surprised then to find the people flocking to Jesus, and he again teaching them.

At once his old enemies, the Pharisees, come to trip him up in his teaching. Up to the very end we shall find Jesus hounded by his enemies, seeking to turn the pilgrims against him. They ask him, " Is it lawful for a man to put away his wife? " Jesus answers them by turning them back to their scriptures. " What did Moses command you? " Moses had not commanded, but he had permitted divorce. " Moses suffered to write a bill of divorcement, and to put her away." But Jesus would penetrate farther back to that which had occasioned Moses' permission. " For the hardness of your heart he wrote you this precept." The permission from Moses was still not the commandment of God, but only at best an accommodation to their hardness of heart — their sinful disobedience to God's will and purposes.

Jesus would have them turn, not to the letter of the Mosaic law, but to go behind the law to the heart and mind of God himself. It is not so much a matter of what the law suffers and permits, but rather of what God desires. " But from the beginning of the creation God made them male and female. For this cause shall a man leave his father and mother, and cleave to his wife; and they twain shall be one flesh. What therefore God hath joined together, let not man put asunder." Here we have very definitive teaching from Jesus concerning marriage, a teaching rooted in Jesus' perception of the purposes of God.

Marriage is a high vocation from God, and not simply a human relationship, having no necessary relation to God. Sex is of God's own creation and is intended to be the instrument through which God himself creates new lives. The sexual act is therefore never simply a human act, but at the same time also an act of God, in and through which God creates and redeems. The sexual nature of man and woman is such that in it there is inevitably involved a physical and spiritual interpenetration of one another, a self-giving whereby an individual ceases to be an individual and becomes abidingly united with the other. Part of oneself lives in the other, physically and spiritually, through the sexual action. Because of this mutual indwelling, one can no longer think of oneself as belonging exclusively to oneself. The man has given himself to the woman and she to him; and that which has been given can never be taken back. One loses the possession and ownership of oneself and comes abidingly under the ownership of the other through this act. It is to this mutual indwelling and belonging that the words " what therefore God hath joined together " refer, and not simply to the fact that God has led this particular man to this particular woman. Man is not to presume to put asunder, to sever, to break that which by biological and spiritual creation God has purposed and enjoined to be one, forever and forever. Jesus' teaching here is not at all rooted in sociology, in that which is for merely social harmony; but rather is rooted in God and his purposes. How often today we try to solve the problems of marriage on a level very different from that of Jesus. So often we ignore God, apart from whom no solution can ever be achieved.

The church's task is to proclaim the high, unconditioned purposes of God for sex and marriage. The church is disloyal to its Teacher and Lord when it seeks to base marriage upon legalisms, the traditions of men — sinful men. With those who fail to live up to the high calling of God for marriage or sex, the church must then exercise her Master's example and practice of repentance and of forgiveness. Each case must be dealt with, not on the basis of legalism, but of redeeming and forgiving love. Only so shall we today be the followers and messengers of Jesus.

43 LITTLE CHILDREN

And they brought young children to him, that he should touch them: and his disciples rebuked those that brought them. But when Jesus saw it, he was much displeased, and said unto them, Suffer the little children to come unto me, and forbid them not: for of such is the kingdom of God. Verily I say unto you, Whosoever shall not receive the kingdom of God as a little child, he shall not enter therein. And he took them up in his arms, put his hands upon them, and blessed them.

Mark 10: 13-16

In good faith, the disciples believed that they were serving Jesus by sheltering him from these parents who brought their children to Jesus for his blessing. The disciples knew that Jesus had weighty matters upon his mind and heart, and this was surely no time for parents to bother him with their little children. Jesus did have heavy matters upon his heart, far more than any of his disciples were able to grasp. Yet he was not so preoccupied with his coming death at Jerusalem that he would not respond lovingly and compassionately to the simple petition of these parents.

We find Jesus, as was his custom, giving more than was asked of him. All that the parents desired or expected was that Jesus would touch their little children with his hand. That would be enough. Jesus did that; in addition he took them one by one into his arms and blessed them. How the hearts of the parents must have rejoiced at this very evident mark of Jesus' care and love for their children.

"Receive the kingdom of God." How hard it is for us today, as for them then, to believe with our whole heart and mind that the Kingdom is given to us as a gift, and not earned and achieved by our human efforts and works. We do not make the kingdom of God, and never can we claim entrance into it by anything that we may ever do. The graciousness of God alone gives us the Kingdom. It is humbling, and even humiliating, to have to receive it as a little child has to receive parental care. We are unable to contribute anything more than our willingness to receive it from God's hands. Only the truly repentant can be humble enough to receive it as a gift.

44 A RICH YOUNG RULER

And when he was gone forth into the way, there came one running, and kneeled to him, and asked him, Good Master, what shall I do that I may inherit eternal life? And Jesus said unto him, Why callest thou me good? there is none good but one, that is, God. Thou knowest the commandments,

> Do not commit adultery,
> Do not kill,
> Do not steal,
> Do not bear false witness,
> Defraud not,
> Honour thy father and mother.

And he answered and said unto him, Master, all these have I observed from my youth. Then Jesus beholding him loved him, and said unto him, One thing thou lackest: go thy way, sell whatsoever thou hast, and give to the poor, and thou shalt have treasure in heaven: and come, take up the cross, and follow me. And he was sad at that saying, and went away grieved: for he had great possessions.

Mark 10: 17-22

This event is closely linked with the preceding one. The young man (we presume him still to be young from his sincere and frank claim to have kept the Law) had perhaps watched the little children receiving the kingdom of God by the mere and simple act of Jesus taking them into his arms and laying his hands upon them. That was a much easier way of entering the Kingdom than the way set forth by the Pharisees. This religious teacher was a kindly person, very different from the stern Pharisees. It was all very well for little children to receive the Kingdom, doing nothing themselves to earn or deserve it; but surely this teacher would give him some task to do, whereby he might win his way into the Kingdom. And Jesus will tell him something to do, and that will be the one thing that he could not do.

Jesus perceived in the question of this young man a turning away from the severity and firmness of God. Jesus could not tolerate for an instant any hint that he was a substitute for God, a refuge away from God, who alone was good. He therefore points the young man at once away from himself, back to God and to the commandments of God. God's commandments can't be broken or altered, even by him. There is no salvation apart from those commandments. Externally the young man might claim to have kept the commandments. Youth and immaturity might well have prompted such a reply.

Jesus, however, saw that despite his external obedience to the commandments the young man's heart was not at rest. He hungered after that which mere external obedience to the law could never give — the friendship of God given through a person, and that person himself. "One thing thou lackest . . ." the need to be freed from his attachments to all earthly possessions, and so be free to receive the gift that Jesus offered him — companionship with him during those great and decisive days which will show forth the very heart of God's love for men. In return for earthly, perishable treasure, Jesus offers heavenly, abiding riches. That offer the young man refused. The possessions of earth were so real and tangible; the things of heaven so ephemeral.

Jesus, however, did not despair even of this young man, making his great refusal. Jesus' faith rested not in men, but in God; not in men's willingness to receive, but in God's unwearied, ever patient will to give salvation.

45 ENTRANCE INTO THE KINGDOM

And Jesus looked round about, and saith unto his disciples, How hardly shall they that have riches enter into the kingdom of God!

It is easier for a camel to go through the eye of a needle, than for a rich man to enter into the kingdom of God.

And the disciples were astonished at his words. But Jesus answereth again, . . . Children, how hard is it . . . to enter into the kingdom of God!

And they were astonished out of measure, saying among themselves, Who then can be saved? And Jesus looking upon them saith, With men it is impossible, but not with God: for with God all things are possible.

Mark 10: 23, 25, 24, 26-27

Liberty has been taken in this passage of transposing the order of verses 24 and 25, and also of omitting the words " for them that trust in riches." The change is not supported by any manuscript evidence, but nevertheless is required to enable us to understand the increasing amazement of the disciples.

Jesus' statement that " it is hard for those having riches to enter the kingdom of God " might well be accepted by the disciples. It might be hard for the rich, but it was not impossible. And at any rate, that saying of Jesus did not apply to any of them, for none of them had great possessions. But when Jesus added to that saying a further one, " It is easier for a camel to go through the eye of a needle, than for a rich man to enter into the kingdom of God," that made it forever impossible for any rich man ever to enter the Kingdom.

Christian scribes have ever since busied themselves with trying to explain the radicalism of Jesus' assertion here. In the first place they have added what they thought must have been his real intention, though by him left unsaid, i.e., " impossible for those who trust in their riches." Other scribes have sought persistently to explain away the ludicrous idea of a camel struggling to squeeze itself through the eye of a needle by claiming that the " eye of a needle " must refer to a special, narrow gate to a city, through which a camel could with effort squeeze.

They seem to have forgotten that on another occasion Jesus used the imagery of a camel under conditions equally fantastic — " straining at a gnat, and swallowing a camel."

The whole point of Jesus' saying here lies in the sheer impossibility — not the difficulty — of entering into the kingdom of God. Our trouble is that we, unlike Jesus, do not believe it is impossible for us to enter into the kingdom of God by our own efforts. To make the impossibility absolute, Jesus then proceeded to utter another saying, which threw the disciples into even greater consternation: " Children, how hard is it to enter into the kingdom of God! " Hard, not only for the rich man, but for anybody, rich or poor, high or low, ignorant or wise, child or adult. Equally hard for all!

This hard dictum Jesus then confirms by his next saying, " With men it is impossible, but not with God." Entrance into the Kingdom is never man's achievement, but God's gracious gift. There is something in all of us which makes us presume to think that we can pay for, or earn our way into the Kingdom — by knowledge, good works, effort, or discipline. But the possibility of our ever arriving in that Kingdom lies wholly with God, not with us. God is not limited by man's impossibilities. Until a man is utterly set free from every dim presumption that he can by his own efforts enter that Kingdom, he does not rightly envisage the reign of God.

46 REWARDS

Then Peter began to say unto him, Lo, we have left all, and have followed thee. And Jesus answered and said, Verily I say unto you, There is no man that hath left house, or brethren, or sisters, or father, or mother, or wife, or children, or lands, for my sake, and the gospel's, but he shall receive an hundredfold now in this time, houses, and brethren, and sisters, and mothers, and children, and lands, with persecutions; and in the world to come eternal life. But many that are first shall be last; and the last first.

Mark 10: 28-31

Invariably when Peter speaks, he speaks amiss. Peter still had a home, wife, children, and a livelihood in the fishing business, to which he could always turn back. We shall later find Peter returned to his family, and fishing on the resurrection morning.

Jesus concerns himself not with correcting Peter's overstatement of his own sacrifice, but with a very different matter. All earthly goods — home, kindred, possessions — all of these, when compared with what God offered to them here and now in this wondrous friendship with Jesus, count as nothing. And when one considers that which is to come from God in the world to come — eternal life with God — then earthly treasures count very little by comparison. No Christian, whatsoever renunciations he may be called upon to make for Jesus' sake, ever counts himself to be a loser. That which God gives far surpasses all that God takes away.

47 DEATH AHEAD

And they were in the way going up to Jerusalem; and Jesus went before them: and they were amazed; and as they followed, they were afraid. And he took again the twelve, and began to tell them what things should happen unto him, saying, Behold, we go up to Jerusalem; and the Son of Man shall be delivered unto the chief priests, and unto the scribes; and they shall condemn him to death, and shall deliver him to the Gentiles: and they shall mock him, and shall scourge him, and shall spit upon him, and shall kill him: and the third day he shall rise again.

Mark 10: 32-34

The fact that Jesus walked ahead, and the disciples followed behind, is symbolic of an isolation and separation that is inner and spiritual. Ever since Jesus had taught them of a *suffering* Messiah and of his own coming death, they had steadfastly resisted that teaching. To their dulled minds and hardened hearts this seemed foolishness and an utter impossibility. If Jesus were the Messiah of God, then it was not even conceivable that he could either suffer or die.

That their minds and hearts shut out this new teaching meant that a gulf had opened between them and Jesus. Their minds were not meeting on common ground. Jesus walked alone on the pathway appointed for him by God; they followed him, unwillingly, without understanding, without oneness of spirit. They were afraid.

Some dim, vague sense that a crisis and tragedy were looming ahead took possession of them. That they faced this crisis separated in will and thought from Jesus filled them with fear and they were all the more fearful because they could not understand it.

Once again Jesus utters that clear warning of what lies ahead for him at Jerusalem. He went up to the Holy City, not to ascertain whether or not the religious leaders there would accept him. Jesus had already had dealings with the superior scribes and Pharisees from Jerusalem. Jesus had already accepted by anticipation the end — the cross. In the wilderness temptations he had first foreseen and accepted the cost of unswerving obedience to God. On the Mount of Transfiguration, Moses and Elijah had conversed with him concerning the ordeal that he was about to undergo at Jerusalem. Jesus had fully and wholly accepted God's vocation for him — that of a suffering, rejected, crucified Messiah.

Jesus' concern now was not for himself, but for his disciples, that they too should accept that destiny for him. That, they steadfastly refused to do. It meant, therefore, that Jesus had to walk the way to the cross, even at that distance, *alone*, without the help or sympathy or companionship of his friends. Long ago he had accepted the loss of any family understanding.

Deeply rooted in the memory of the disciples after the resurrection was the consciousness that Jesus, not once but repeatedly, had forewarned them of the end. Equally vivid in their memories was their persistent inability to grasp or accept those warnings.

48 SELF-SEEKING

James and John, the sons of Zebedee, come unto him, saying, Master, we would that thou shouldest do for us whatsoever we shall desire. And he said unto them, What would ye that I should do for you? They said unto him, Grant unto us that we may sit, one on thy right hand, and the other on thy left hand, in thy glory. But Jesus said unto them, Ye know not what ye ask: can ye drink of the cup that I drink of? and be baptized with the baptism that I am baptized with? And they said unto him, We can. And Jesus said unto them, Ye shall indeed drink of the cup that I drink of; and with the baptism that I am baptized withal shall ye be baptized: but to sit on my right hand and on my left hand is not mine to give; but it shall be given to them for whom it is prepared.

Mark 10: 35-40

For at least one year, and possibly as long as three, the disciples had accompanied Jesus. They had lived with him, watched him, heard him. Now with less than two weeks remaining of earthly life for Jesus, so little had they grasped the significance of his teaching concerning the kingdom of God, that two of them (and those two from the innermost circle of his friends) could come to him, seeking to gain for themselves places of pre-eminence in the earthly kingdom they were still anticipating. They supposed Jesus was going up to Jerusalem to inaugurate an earthly kingdom, with himself as earthly king. For themselves they sought the two highest positions — those of prime minister and treasurer, perhaps.

The two disciples had however grasped enough of Jesus' spirit and teaching to know that their request could only be obtained from him by concealing its exact nature. " Master, we would that thou shouldest do for us whatsoever we shall desire." No petition could be further away from the spirit of prayer that Jesus had given them — " Our Father . . . *thy* will be done." John and James preferred to pray, " *Our* will be done." And who are we to judge or rebuke them?

Jesus might have rebuked them, and done so bitterly, in despair at the slowness of understanding and at the unabashed selfishness of these two closest friends. Instead he patiently and courteously leads them on to his refusal of their petition. " Ye ask amiss." How true are those words! Who else but Jesus could have made the refusal in such a loving way? He leads them by his own question to make explicit and open their hidden desire. Jesus then states (and what deep understanding and forgiveness lie in his words), " Ye know not what ye ask." No, not even after that period of training under him did they know what they were doing. These are the same words that Jesus will utter from the cross on behalf of those who were crucifying him, " Father, forgive them, for they know not what they do."

The Greek verbs in this section should properly be translated not as " I drink of," but as " I *am drinking* of."[1] Already by anticipation Jesus is revealed to us as drinking the cup of the passion. Every step of the way up to Jerusalem held up before his imagination the vision of the cross. He was under no delusions as to what lay in store for him in the Holy City of God.

" Not mine to give." Jesus did not rob God of the divine prerogatives. The places of honor in that Kingdom are not secured by running for election; they are appointed by God. We know that the position on the right hand of God in the Kingdom was appointed for Jesus. We still do not know for whom the place on God's left is appointed. Jesus would not even ask for himself the place on God's right hand. He is there, not by his own request, but by God's appointment.

49 JEALOUSY

When the ten heard it, they began to be much displeased with James and John. But Jesus called them to him, and saith unto them, Ye know that they which are accounted to rule over the Gentiles exercise lordship over them; and their great ones exercise authority upon them. But so shall

[1] See Mark 10 : 38 in *The Complete Bible, an American Translation,* translated by J. M. Powis Smith and Edgar J. Goodspeed. University of Chicago Press.

it not be among you: but whosoever . . . of you will be the chiefest, shall be servant of all. For even the Son of Man came not to be ministered unto, but to minister, and to give his life a ransom for many.

Mark 10: 41-45

We can readily understand the jealousy and indignation of the ten against James and John. But their own jealousy and anger against the two in itself indicates their own lack of compassion and understanding. We wonder and are amazed at the unwearied patience of Jesus in dealing with his chosen disciples. Never does he despair of them, not even in the midst of their very failures. His trust in them was not rooted in that which they already were, but in that which God could do with them through the mighty power of forgiving love.

Jesus gives a *loving correction* to the whole apostolic band, a teaching fully exemplified in his own life — the role of servanthood, accepted and lived humbly, voluntarily, lovingly. The world counts greatness by the measure of being served. Jesus holds up to his disciples, and to us today, a very different measure of greatness. He is truly great who can do most for the blessing of others. Jesus himself came not to be served by men, but to be a servant unto them.

"To give his life a ransom for many." Here we are given by Jesus his own interpretation of his vocation. His is a vicarious ministry. By his acts the lives of others are to be set free from self-seeking, that life in which man can never know God's peace. And to our query, "Are there few that be saved?" we have Jesus' own reply that he is giving his life a ransom for *many*.

50 NOW OR NEVER

Another of his disciples said unto him, Sir, suffer me first to go and bury my father. But Jesus said unto him, Follow me; and let the dead bury their dead.

Matthew 8: 21-22

As this event is placed in the Gospel as written by Matthew, we are at a loss to understand the severity of Jesus' demand upon this would-be follower. If, however, we place it here at this stage of Jesus' ministry, we are enabled to make it have significant meaning.

Oriental funeral customs often demanded many days of entertainment of guests. Jesus knew that if this man was to follow him, it must be now or never. By the time that the man would be free from family responsibilities connected with his father's burial, and would be free to follow him to Jerusalem, Jesus himself would have been crucified. For this particular disciple, then, it meant the stark necessity of following Jesus at once, even at the cost of neglecting an elemental duty to his father and family.

51 ZACCHAEUS

And they came to Jericho. . . .

And, behold, there was a man named Zacchaeus, which was the chief among the publicans, and he was rich. And he sought to see Jesus who he was; and could not for the press, because he was little of stature. And he ran before, and climbed up into a sycamore tree to see him: for he was to pass that way.

And when Jesus came to the place, he looked up, and saw him, and said unto him, Zacchaeus, make haste, and come down; for today I must abide at thy house. And he made haste, and came down, and received him joyfully.

And when they saw it, they all murmured, saying, That he was gone to be guest with a man that is a sinner. And Zacchaeus stood, and said unto Jesus; Behold, Jesus, the half of my goods I give to the poor; and if I have taken any thing from any man by false accusation, I restore him fourfold. And Jesus said unto him, This day is salvation come to this house, forsomuch as he also is a son of Abraham. For the Son of Man is come to seek and to save that which was lost.

Mark 10: 46 and Luke 19: 2-10

We are inclined to believe that Matthew had a large part to play in this meeting between Jesus and Zacchaeus. It may well have been that during his days as a tax collector for the Romans at Capernaum, Matthew had had both business dealings and friendship with Zacchaeus, the chief of the tax collectors. What would seem more likely than that Matthew had been writing from time to time to Zacchaeus of his wondrous new friendship with Jesus, and of the mighty deeds and new teaching of Jesus in Galilee. Something in Zacchaeus hungered for such a friendship; but any likelihood of its happening to him seemed very remote, if not utterly impossible.

Zacchaeus was rich, but he was also very lonely. He knew that almost every Jew in Jericho hated and despised him as a traitor to Jewish nationalism. If not formally excommunicate from the Jericho synagogues, yet he knew that he would never be welcomed there, and so for all practical purposes he was a religious outcast. It is very hard to believe in the friendship of God, when the servants of that God show only hatred and animosity. Zacchaeus had an additional handicap, hard to bear — he was unusually short of stature. It meant that whenever he had to talk to people, they would look down upon him. So easily this physical fact would breed self-consciousness and a sense of inferiority.

Perhaps Matthew had written Zacchaeus that Jesus was soon to pass through Jericho on his way to Jerusalem. Or it may rather have been nothing more than the report brought by the advance pilgrims, that Jesus was on the road. Rumors of his teaching, mighty works, and conflicts with the Pharisees would certainly have spread to Jericho; and the people of that city would be eager for his arrival. The most that Zacchaeus hoped for or desired was a very little thing — merely that he might with his eyes behold Jesus as he passed by on the road. It never occurred to him that something far different was in store for him.

It soon appeared certain, however, that his hope to see Jesus passing by would be denied him. The roadside was thronged with crowds of people, and he, with his short stature, could never hope to get a glimpse of Jesus over the heads of all these people. And when he tried to push his way into the front ranks, we can be sure he was pushed back roughly. But there was a spirit of determination in Zacchaeus. How the children and adults of Jericho must have jeered and jibed as they watched Zacchaeus in his desperation clumsily climbing up into a nearby sycamore tree. But his deep desire to see Jesus overweighed his fear of the jeers of the multitude, and when Jesus did come by, Zacchaeus looked down from amidst the leafy branches upon him.

It is noteworthy that Jesus calls Zacchaeus by name. We presume, therefore, that Matthew had told Jesus something about his lonely, publican friend at Jericho. Jesus looked up into the eyes of Zacchaeus, and read there his wistful, unspoken hunger after companionship. At once he acted in compassion to meet that deep and tragic need. Jesus bade him come down with haste, that he might sojourn that day in his home.

We might well have expected that on this last sabbath weekend before his death Jesus would have wanted to be alone in retreat, alone with God and with his little band of disciples. But Jesus never took concern for himself while there were others whose needs were to be met. He was always so preoccupied with the needs of others that there was no time left to take concern for himself.

How Zacchaeus' heart must have burst with this unasked-for joy! All that he had hoped for was to see Jesus as he passed by on the road. That would have been enough. Now this same Jesus had invited him to be his host over the sabbath. Jesus always gave far better things than men asked for. Men ask so little; God gives so much.

We would give much to know what Jesus and Zacchaeus talked of during Jesus' stay in his home. The Gospels as usual are very reticent in revealing the innermost secrets of human hearts. We presume that there was but one thing of which Jesus would talk — God and God's kingdom.

52 BARTIMAEUS

As he went out of Jericho with his disciples and a great number of people, blind Bartimaeus, the son of Timaeus, sat by the highway side begging. And when he heard that it was Jesus of Nazareth, he began to cry out, and say, Jesus, thou son of David, have mercy on me. And many charged him that he should hold his peace: but he cried the more a great deal, Thou son of David, have mercy on me.

And Jesus stood still, and commanded him to be called. And they call the blind man, saying unto him, Be of good comfort, rise; he calleth thee. And he, casting away his garment, rose, and came to Jesus. And Jesus answered and said unto him, What wilt thou that I should do unto thee? The blind man said unto him, Sir, that I might receive my sight. And Jesus said unto him, Go thy way; thy faith hath made thee whole. And immediately he received his sight, and followed Jesus in the way.

Mark 10: 46-52

After the sabbath day weekend the road would be thronged with pilgrims going up to the feast at Jerusalem. The crowds would be especially great this day because of the event connected with Zacchaeus. On every lip would be the name of Jesus of Nazareth. A blind beggar of Jericho — perhaps a professional beggar — counted this an opportunity of getting alms for himself. As Jesus comes and the crowd murmurs his name, the beggar feels impelled to seek an alms from this Jesus. Perhaps he had heard echoes of the mighty works which Jesus had performed in Galilee. So at once he breaks forth into his beggar's litany, " Jesus, son of David, have mercy on me." Not once, but repeatedly, he kept crying his plea.

Amidst all the stir and shoutings of the multitude beside the road Jesus' ear picked up the whine of the beggar, hidden in the crowd. Jesus could not distinguish who was uttering the cry, nor could he call him by name, for he knew it not. He stopped therefore and asked the people to bring the beggar to him. The way in which the beggar threw off his cloak, and rushed up to Jesus, would almost lead the people to doubt his blindness. " What wilt thou that I should do unto thee? "

The beggar in reply strangely found his lips saying, " Sir, that I might receive my sight." Did the beggar's request come as a surprise even to himself? He had never before asked this of any passer-by, but only alms. His stupendous plea came to his lips rather as something said by another. They were his own words, and yet also not his own, but words spoken by another through him. Is that what we mean by faith in a person — that one finds himself saying and doing that which he has mysteriously received from another?

This is the only miracle that Jesus performs in this part of his ministry. Hitherto in Galilee he had done his mighty works in secret, unwilling that men should report them to others. But in this case Jesus was determined to enter Jerusalem with acclaim, not secretly or silently.

We must not read into the beggar's address " son of David " any Messianic significance. Where even the crowd of pilgrims had no inkling that this Jesus was anything more than a prophet from Nazareth, and the secret of Jesus being the Messiah of God was known only to the twelve and they sworn to secrecy concerning it, we are certainly not to believe that this beggar knew Jesus as the Messiah. The term is simply the beggar's art, hoping by the use of that honorable title to secure his attention. The crowd paid no attention to his cry as being anything more than a beggar's chant.

PART SIX

JERUSALEM

53 ENTRANCE INTO JERUSALEM

When they came nigh to Jerusalem, unto Bethphage and Bethany, at the mount of Olives, he sendeth forth two of his disciples, and saith unto them, Go your way into the village over against you: and as soon as ye be entered into it, ye shall find a colt tied, whereon never man sat; loose him, and bring him. And if any man say unto you, Why do ye this? say ye that I have need of him; and straightway he will send him hither.

And they went their way, and found the colt . . . without in a place where two ways met; and they loose him. And certain of them that stood there said unto them, What do ye, loosing the colt? And they said unto them even as Jesus had commanded: and they let them go.

And they brought the colt to Jesus, and cast their garments on him; and he sat upon him. And many spread their garments in the way; and others cut down branches off the trees, and strewed them in the way. And they that went before, and they that followed, cried, saying, Hosanna; Blessed is he that cometh in the name of the Lord: Blessed be the kingdom of our father David, that cometh in the name of the Lord: Hosanna in the highest.

And Jesus entered into Jerusalem, and into the temple: and when he had looked round about upon all things, and now the eventide was come, he went out unto Bethany with the twelve.

Mark 11: 1-11

We, who read the Gospels with the preconception that Jesus is God's Messiah, are naturally prone to interpret the ovation to Jesus upon entering Jerusalem as a Messianic welcome. Matthew, in his account of this event, writes of the acclaim as being made to "the son of David"; Luke has it as "Blessed be the King that cometh in the name of God." John in his account indicates it to be a Messianic welcome. But if the perspective of Mark is authentic, and the Messianic secret is known to none but the twelve disciples, then it is evident that this ovation cannot be a Messianic one. Matthew's account is not in itself consistent, for he also records that when the people of Jerusalem ask who this person Jesus is, the pilgrims reply that it is " Jesus, the prophet of Nazareth."

It seems very probable that the people of Jerusalem had nothing to do with this ovation. Rather it is the pilgrims of Galilee who take part in it. Let us try then to understand this event from the historical perspective which Mark gives.

Although Jesus had walked the distance from Galilee to the Mount of Olives, yet when he reached Bethany he secured a colt and descended the Mount of Olives, riding upon it into the city. This is for Jesus his last entry into the Holy City, and it is to be made memorable. Thus he enters the city with dignity, but it is the dignity of a prophet, rather than of a Messianic king. Popular conceptions of the Messiah did not include the lowly picture of a Messiah riding humbly upon a colt.

The branches are to be thought of as the small branches of the low bushes from the side of the road. The only trees available would be the orchard fruit trees, and it is very unlikely that the orchard owners would tolerate the pilgrims stripping them of their branches. We picture then the Galilean pilgrims, with their realization that this is an unusual entrance into the city on the part of their prophet from Galilee. They had no deeper understanding of it than that. Gathering from the roadside flowers and grasses, and small branches from the shrubs and bushes, they strew them before the colt on which Jesus was seated, and cried out their pilgrim songs in honor of the coming Messianic age, but with no thought that Jesus was the Messiah.

The Gospels do not inform us of the mystery of how the colt is secured upon the mere request of two disciples; but we can be sure that any rationalization on our part is not likely to be a true one. It is not necessary that we should know.

We take for granted that during the days of the feast Jesus

and his disciples camped out near Bethany; each day going into the city to the temple, and each night withdrawing to some orchard to spend the night. We who do not make religious pilgrimages have perhaps never known the joy and excitement of pilgrim life. Orchard owners would be glad to have little bands of pilgrims camp on their property, for it gave them a chance to sell them provisions and to have friendly gossip with them.

54 CLEANSING THE TEMPLE

And they come to Jerusalem: and Jesus went into the temple, and began to cast out them that sold and bought in the temple, and overthrew the tables of the moneychangers, and the seats of them that sold doves; and would not suffer that any man should carry any vessel through the temple. And he taught, saying unto them, Is it not written, My house shall be called of all nations the house of prayer? but ye have made it a den of thieves. And the scribes and chief priests heard it, and sought how they might destroy him: for they feared him, because all the people was astonished at his doctrine. And when even was come, he went out of the city.

Mark 11: 15-19

It is one thing to read in a book about sacrifice; it is quite another matter to witness it. The modern city abattoir would give us some comprehension of what went on in the temple precincts during a major religious feast. There would be the piteous bleating of the lambs, the frightened bellowing of the bullocks, the cries of the doves in their cages; blood smearing the floor and the white garments of the priests; the water carriers carrying their buckets of water through the temple courtyards. Many a pilgrim, who had made the long journey to the temple for the feast, the very heart and center of Judaism, must have felt nothing but disillusionment and disgust at the whole traffic. Yet none dared to speak or act against it all.

It was customary at the great feasts for the pilgrims to pay in person their annual temple poll tax, as well as to make special thank offerings. To do so required the exchange of Roman currency into special temple money. That meant the need for money-changers, with the consequent haggling over rates of exchange. It must have been exceedingly difficult, if not utterly impossible, to find God there amid the confusion and tumult of the temple.

Only Jesus dared to act against all of this. We completely miss the whole point of this event, if we picture Jesus, with a whip of cords, in his anger whipping both cattle and people out of the temple. Such a picture cannot be historic. In the first place, the temple police could instantly have overpowered Jesus. No lonely figure, armed with a scourge of cords, could for a moment have held the temple authorities immobile.

The force which Jesus exercised was not physical, but moral and spiritual. His daring statement, " My house shall be called of all nations the house of prayer; but ye have made it a den of thieves," had struck home to the hearts of all who heard him. Every man there, priest or pilgrim, knew that Jesus spoke truth. The temple was a den of thieves; it ought to be a house of prayer, and was not. It was the unchallengeable truth of Jesus' words that made any physical action against him on the part of the temple authorities utterly impossible.

The stunned reaction was not long-lasting. We can well believe that next morning the temple traffic was back again in full swing, with extra temple police on the alert to prevent any recurrence of yesterday's incident. But Jesus will utter a second and last word concerning the temple. To his disciples, deeply impressed by the massive temple architecture, Jesus will say, " Seest thou these great buildings? There shall not be left one stone upon another, that shall not be thrown down." A temple that will not be cleansed, so that it may truly become a house of prayer for all nations, must then be destroyed.

This act of Jesus was a daring, provocative one, and we shall

expect that the temple authorities will react violently against
him for it. In the presence of the crowds of pilgrims they dared
not act, but they will find a time and an occasion when they
can seize Jesus and wreak upon him their will.

55 AUTHORITY

And they come again to Jerusalem: and as he was walking in the temple,
there come to him the chief priests, and the scribes, and the elders, and
say unto him, By what authority doest thou these things? and who
gave thee this authority to do these things? And Jesus answered and
said unto them, I will also ask of you one question, and answer me, and
I will tell you by what authority I do these things. The baptism of John,
was it from heaven, or of men? answer me.

And they reasoned with themselves, saying, If we shall say, From
heaven; he will say, Why then did ye not believe him? But if we shall say,
Of men; they feared the people: for all men counted John, that he was a
prophet indeed. And they answered and said unto Jesus, We cannot tell.
And Jesus answering saith unto them, Neither do I tell you by what
authority I do these things.

Mark 11: 27-33

We expected that there would be a sequel to Jesus' act of
cleansing the temple, and here it is given to us. A delegation of
chief priests, scribes, and elders seek out Jesus in the temple
courts and demand to know by what authority he has dared to
do this provocative act in the temple of God.

Confronted with the highest religious authority of Judaism,
Jesus shows himself complete master of the situation. Following his custom, Jesus meets question with question, and that a
question which pierces deeply to the very heart of the matter.
His question will convict them of sin.

What have they to say regarding the baptism of John — the
baptism of repentance? Had they been willing to accept John's
call to repent, they would not now be asking their question of
Jesus, for they themselves, in the vision and power of true
repentance, would long ago have cleansed the temple. If they
answered Jesus that the baptism of John was an act initiated by
God to lead men into God's forgiveness, then Jesus would

demand of them why they had not brought forth the fruits of true repentance as John had demanded. If they answered Jesus that the baptism of John was of men, they would at once have to face the indignation and hostility of the pilgrim crowds, and the temple trade would suffer.

Their reply — "We cannot tell" — really means that they *refuse* to answer Jesus. The answer of Jesus is most significant. To those who have not met the precondition of true repentance, the only answer Jesus could give would be meaningless. Previously some of these same Jerusalem scribes had evaluated his work in Galilee as the work of Beelzebul. Then he had told them that he did his mighty works by "the finger of God." They are not ready for any further answer than that. Jesus' secret of being the Messiah is still known only to the little band of twelve disciples.

56 PARABLE OF THE VINEYARD

And he began to speak unto them by parables. A certain man planted a vineyard, and set an hedge about it, and digged a place for the winefat, and built a tower, and let it out to husbandmen, and went into a far country. And at the season he sent to the husbandmen a servant, that he might receive from the husbandmen of the fruit of the vineyard. And they caught him, and beat him, and sent him away empty.

And again he sent unto them another servant; and at him they cast stones, and wounded him in the head, and sent him away shamefully handled. And again he sent another; and him they killed, and many others; beating some, and killing some.

Having yet therefore one son, his well-beloved, he sent him also last unto them, saying, They will reverence my son. But those husbandmen said among themselves, This is the heir; come, let us kill him, and the inheritance shall be ours. And they took him, and killed him, and cast him out of the vineyard. What shall therefore the lord of the vineyard do? he will come and destroy the husbandmen, and will give the vineyard unto others. And have ye not read this scripture; The stone which the builders rejected is become the head of the corner: This was the Lord's doing, and it is marvellous in our eyes?

And they sought to lay hold on him, but feared the people: for they knew that he had spoken the parable against them: and they left him, and went their way.

Mark 12: 1-12

In this parable we find for the third time now the usage of that key word *agapetos*, translated here as " well-beloved." As in the two previous cases (the Baptism and the Transfiguration) we shall expect this passage to contain an important insight into the person Jesus.

The imagery of God's people as a vineyard is one which was repeatedly used in the scriptures of Judaism. As Jesus uses the imagery here, the vineyard owner is God; the servants are the prophets whom God has sent again and again to his people. The unwearied persistence of God in the face of the repeated rejection of his servants tells us much concerning his loving patience. God will not abandon his people, despite their hardened sinning against him.

After the sending of his servants, all to no avail, God at last sends his only Son, his well-beloved. Here we are given by Jesus his own self-consciousness that his own status with God was not that of a servant-prophet, but of a Son — an *only* Son. Jesus does not rank himself in the same class as the prophets of old. His status is unique, and not to be compared to that of those who had come before him.

Here too we are given by Jesus the prophecy of his fast-approaching death. He has already by anticipation accepted his coming rejection and death at the hands of the Jewish religious authorities; and combined with it he also reveals to us his trust and hope that God will use his death to bring into being a new religious fellowship — that which will be known as the Christian Church. Here, as perhaps nowhere else in the Gospels, we find the prophecy of the inevitable schism which will come, separating Christianity forever from Judaism.

Only through fear of the people were the authorities restrained from laying hands upon Jesus. They saw all too clearly the meaning of his parable. Their will to destroy Jesus is here; all that is lacking is the occasion in which to carry out their intent to kill him.

57 GOD AND CAESAR

They send unto him certain of the Pharisees and of the Herodians, to catch him in his words. And when they were come, they say unto him, Master, we know that thou art true, and carest for no man: for thou regardest not the person of men, but teachest the way of God in truth: Is it lawful to give tribute to Caesar, or not? Shall we give, or shall we not give? But he, knowing their hypocrisy, said unto them, Why tempt ye me? bring me a penny, that I may see it. And they brought it. And he saith unto them, Whose is this image and superscription? And they said unto him, Caesar's. And Jesus answering said unto them, Render to Caesar the things that are Caesar's, and to God the things that are God's. And they marvelled at him.

Mark 12: 13-17

Both the temple authorities and the Pharisees, despite their many differences, were united upon one end — the destruction of this man Jesus. In this next event it is the Pharisees who seek to trap Jesus and turn the pilgrims against him. So long as he had pilgrim support, they could not openly seize or harm him.

Nothing could be counted upon more surely to turn the pilgrims against Jesus than to trap Jesus in a position in which he would be guilty of lack of Jewish patriotism. The pilgrims who came up to the feast would naturally be those who held strong, nationalist feelings and expectations. During the times of the major feasts, the tide of Jewish nationalism ran strong, and extra Roman troops were brought up from Caesarea to be ready for all possible contingencies.

Jesus' enemies approached him with a dilemma, confident that no matter how Jesus might reply to it, they could use his answer against him, either with the pilgrims or with the Roman authorities. Openly to assert that it was illegal to pay taxes to the Romans could be used before Pilate as a political charge. On the other hand, to assert before the pilgrim crowds that it was legal to pay taxes to the hated Romans would at once incur the hostility of the pilgrims.

But Jesus was not to be trapped in any dilemma. He was an

unrivaled master of the art of question and answer, for behind him lay all the keen and penetrating wisdom of God. He saw at once the hypocrisy of his enemies. Their desire is not for a clear and unequivocal reply to their question, but rather for an opportunity of ensnaring him. He answers their question with his question, "Why tempt ye me? Bring me a penny, that I may see it." His enemies had no scruples about having a Roman coin in their possession, even here in the temple. On the coin lay visibly engraved the image of Caesar. Unmistakably then the coin belonged to him. Therefore, give it to Caesar.

There are also things which belong unequivocally to God, just as this coin did to Caesar. What are the things that God can rightfully claim from men? What, but repentance, obedience, faith, thankfulness? Let his enemies give those things to God.

We can well understand their marveling at the skillfulness of Jesus in this encounter. Or perhaps it was not the Pharisees who marveled, but the pilgrim onlookers.

58 A WOMAN TAKEN IN ADULTERY

Early in the morning he came again into the temple, and all the people came unto him; and he sat down, and taught them.

And the scribes and Pharisees brought unto him a woman taken in adultery; and when they had set her in the midst, they say unto him, Master, this woman was taken in adultery, in the very act. Now Moses in the law commanded us, that such should be stoned: but what sayest thou? This they said, tempting him, that they might have to accuse him.

But Jesus stooped down and with his finger wrote on the ground, as though he heard them not. So when they continued asking him, he lifted up himself, and said unto them, He that is without sin among you, let him first cast a stone at her.

And again he stooped down, and wrote on the ground. And they which heard it, being convicted by their own conscience, went out one by one, beginning at the eldest, even unto the last: and Jesus was left alone, and the woman standing in the midst. When Jesus had lifted up himself, and saw none but the woman, he said unto her, Woman, where are those thine accusers? hath no man condemned thee? She said, No man, Sir. And Jesus said unto her, Neither do I condemn thee: go, and sin no more.

John 8: 2-11

This event is not recorded in any of the other gospel records. Our earliest Greek manuscripts of John do not contain this story, either. At some later time an unknown copyist must have added this story to the text of John he was copying, deriving it from some source unknown to us. However, we cannot have the slightest doubt of the historical truth of the incident. It fits too well into the story of Jesus' ministry to be challenged as merely imaginative.

The Pharisees had just been worsted in the matter of paying the Roman taxes. But here is a case which they bring to him for which there is definite command from Moses to enact the penalty of stoning. Would Jesus dare to set aside the Mosaic law, and that in the presence of the pilgrim crowd? Would he dare to substitute for the law of Moses his own word of free forgiveness?

We suspect that it was not by accident that the Pharisees had caught this woman in the very act of adultery. It may very well have been an " arranged case." At any rate, the male partner to the act of adultery is notably absent.

We can readily picture the shame and confusion of the unfortunate woman, as she is dragged into the midst of these men, who leer and gloat over her sin with lewd eyes, in which there was no trace of pity or compassion. No matter where she turned her gaze, there was no escape from the eyes of these men.

" Rabbi, this woman was taken in adultery, in the very act. Now Moses in the law commanded us, that such should be stoned; but what sayest thou? " Jesus answers them first by silence. Stooping down from the seat where he had been teaching, with his finger he made movements upon the dirt floor of the temple. There is more to that single action than meets the eye.

We need not believe that there on the dust he wrote out the sins of each individual man. The act has a much deeper significance than that. Jesus' intention was rather one of great and gentlemanly courtesy to the woman. What could serve to take the leering eyes of her accusers from her face and give her a few moments in which to compose herself? What better way than to stoop and silently make marks on the ground? We know that by his action he diverted every eye from the woman. We can also be sure that the woman, if not the men, understood his gracious courtesy.

They were determined to have from Jesus an answer to their question. But the answer that he will give them will be a very different one than they expected or wanted. It is not a word about the woman, but about themselves. "He that is without sin among you, let him first cast a stone at her." Those words are not debatable words. Jesus' questions are often best answered not by the lips, but rather in the deep privacy and silence of the human heart. No longer now were their eyes fastened upon the woman. No man dared to look into Jesus' eyes; and anyway, Jesus had at once again stooped down to write on the ground. He would not do to them that which he had sought to divert them from doing to the woman. Jesus would not embarrass them by looking into their eyes.

That Jesus' words hit home to each man's heart is evidenced by their response. Instead of demanding an answer to their question, they began one by one to leave the scene. At last only Jesus was left, and the woman. Two silent figures. We can picture the woman in wonder gazing at the stooped figure of Jesus. Who is this man who thus mercifully and compassionately deals with her and her sin?

Then Jesus lifted up himself and looked upon the woman. Very different was the look from these eyes from that of the men she had known. The judgment of these eyes was deep and piercing. There was nothing that could be hid from them. Yet wondrously there came with this man's gaze the experience of cleansing and of peace. Here is the mighty experience of forgiveness, conveyed through eyes. No words could have uttered anything more than his gaze did.

"Woman, where are those thine accusers? Hath no man condemned thee?" She said, "No man, Sir." And Jesus said unto her, "Neither do I condemn thee; go, and sin no more." Only a few brief words; no lecture and no scolding. No looking to the past, but rather an entreaty for the future. And the woman knew that this man could be thanked for all his courtesy and compassion only by her going out and sinning no more.

We know of no sequel to this event. The writers of the Gospels did not disclose her identity to us and we must reverence their silence.

59 AN ACADEMIC QUESTION

Then come unto him the Sadducees, which say there is no resurrection; and they asked him, saying, Master, Moses wrote unto us, If a man's brother die, and leave his wife behind him, and leave no children, that his brother should take his wife, and raise up seed unto his brother. Now there were seven brethren: and the first took a wife, and dying left no seed. And the second took her, and died, neither left he any seed: and the third likewise. And the seven had her, and left no seed: last of all the woman died also. In the resurrection therefore, when they shall rise, whose wife shall she be of them? for the seven had her to wife.

And Jesus answering said unto them, Do ye not therefore err, because ye know not the scriptures, neither the power of God? For when they shall rise from the dead, they neither marry, nor are given in marriage; but are as the angels which are in heaven.

And as touching the dead, that they rise: have ye not read in the book of Moses, how in the bush [passage] God spake unto him, saying, I am the God of Abraham, and the God of Isaac, and the God of Jacob? He is not the God of the dead, but the God of the living: ye therefore do greatly err.

Mark 12: 18-27

Twice in quick succession the Pharisees had been defeated in their attempts to trap Jesus. We are not surprised then to find that the temple Sadducees now take their turn in the attempt to confound Jesus.

Whereas the Pharisees had brought real, living issues to Jesus in their questions, this is not so with the question which the Sadducees ask. Their case is beyond all doubt a theoretic, academic question, and therefore one to which no real answer could be given. Such an absurd question originated not from any concrete case, but only from the perverted imagination and speculation of dull-witted scribes. The amazing thing is that to such an unreal question Jesus could give such a deep answer.

The Sadducees professed to have no belief in the resurrection; yet their question is based upon the hypothesis that there is resurrection for all. Jesus gave them a double answer. Jesus accepts unconditionally the premise of their question — that the seven brethren and the woman will rise in the resurrection. But Jesus would correct their gross, materialistic conceptions of the resurrection life. It is in no way a mere perpetuation of this earthly life. Life there is a glorified life, radically different in nature from this earthly life. The very forms of life here — home, marriage, friendship — exist there only in a much changed and purified manner. These Sadducees err greatly in their conception of the resurrection life in merely earthly forms.

They also err greatly, not knowing either the Scriptures or the power of God. Jesus' own faith in resurrection lay not in any speculations upon the immortality of some hidden part of human nature; rather it was grounded in the power of God to give resurrection life. Only when our hope lies *there*, is our trust upon sure foundations. His own faith and hope that after his coming death he would be raised from death was rooted in God.

Jesus then proceeds to find in the Holy Scriptures a " proof " of the resurrection life, and he finds it in a place where no scribe had ever dreamed of looking for it. God's word to Moses was not " I *was* the God of Abraham, and the God of Isaac, and the God of Jacob." Instead it is " I *am*." Jesus himself in the Transfiguration had had the experience of living fellowship with Moses and Elijah. Jesus looked upon these heroes of the Jewish past not as dead heroes, but as living witnesses, watching with deep concern his ministry on earth.

60 THE GREAT COMMANDMENT

And one of the scribes came, and having heard them reasoning together, and perceiving that he had answered them well, asked him, Which is the first commandment of all? And Jesus answered him, The first of all the commandments is, Hear, O Israel; the Lord our God is one Lord: and thou shalt love the Lord thy God with all thy heart, and with all thy soul, and with all thy mind, and with all thy strength: this is the first commandment. And the second is like, namely this, Thou shalt love thy neighbour as thyself. There is none other commandment greater than these.

And the scribe said unto him, Well, Master, thou hast said the truth: for there is one God; and there is none other but he: and to love him with all the heart, and with all the understanding, and with all the soul, and with all the strength, and to love his neighbour as himself, is more than all whole burnt offerings and sacrifices.

And when Jesus saw that he answered discreetly, he said unto him, Thou art not far from the kingdom of God. And no man after that durst ask him any question.

Mark 12: 28-34

This question has about it the ring of sincerity, utterly unlike the questions of Jesus' enemies. Here was an individual scribe, troubled and concerned after religious guidance. In addition to the ten commandments given by God to Moses, there had also grown up some six hundred odd other laws and injunctions of men. It was simply impossible to keep them all. Which of them were to have a man's primary attention? Out of the six hundred laws, which kind or class should have man's first concern? The Greek word used in the scribe's question should rightly be translated " kind " or " class."

The scribe asked at best for a short list of the most important commandments of all. Jesus gave him more than he asked for — a first and greatest commandment, and also a second, like unto the first. Jesus reduced the six hundred odd commandments to but two — something that no scribe before him had ever done.

Jesus in his answer brings together two ancient commandments. The first and great commandment he quotes from Deuteronomy 6: 4-5; the second from Leviticus 19: 18. When we read the source from which the second commandment comes we are amazed. It is like finding a precious jewel in a dump, amidst all the worthless refuse. It shows us that Jesus had in his reading of the Scriptures of his people done real mining, to be able to find this jewel in the midst of so much rubbish. We owe it too to Jesus that for the first time these two separated commandments are joined together. And that which he has joined together, we are not to presume to put asunder. Neither mysticism nor mere humanitarianism are adequate substitutes for this double religious commandment given us by Jesus.

The fact that the scribe willingly and gladly accepts Jesus' discerning evaluation of the law makes us realize that not all scribes were his bitter opponents. A man is not *far* from (yet still not *within*) the Kingdom when he is prepared to live in accordance with this twin standard of life — to love God wholly and unconditionally, and to love his fellow man as himself.

We can also well understand that after these two encounters, none of his enemies for the time being dared to match their wits against Jesus' wisdom from on high.

61 DAVIDIC DESCENT

Jesus answered and said, while he taught in the temple, How say the scribes that Christ is the son of David? For David himself said by the Holy Ghost, The Lord said to my Lord, Sit thou on my right hand, till I make thine enemies thy footstool. David therefore himself calleth him Lord; and whence is he then his son?

And the common people heard him gladly.

Mark 12: 35-37

Jesus knew himself as the Messiah in a heavenly sense. The popular conception held by the people was that Messiah was descended from King David — and was thus an earthly king and would rule an earthly, political kingdom. Jesus would correct their erroneous conception. He knew their Scriptures far more truly and deeply than the doctors of his age. If David himself could speak of the expected Messiah as Lord, such a person could hardly then be conceived of as his human son. Their great hero king, David, then should show them that they were misinterpreting the term *Messiah*. Far more than Davidic descent was required of the Messiah. God, and not David, was to be the origin of the Messiah.

62 GIVING

Jesus sat over against the treasury, and beheld how the people cast money into the treasury: and many that were rich cast in much. And there came a certain poor widow, and she threw in two mites, which make a farthing. And he called unto him his disciples, and saith unto them, Verily I say unto you, That this poor widow hath cast more in, than all they which have cast into the treasury: For all they did cast in of their abundance; but she of her want did cast in all that she had, even all her living.

Mark 12: 41-44

At the time of the great feasts, every Jew was expected to pay his annual poll tax. In addition, provision was made for pilgrims to give thank offerings — gifts over and above that which the law required. Undoubtedly then, as now, such surplus giving won the giver " merit " with God. Let us picture in our imaginations one of the courtyards of the temple, within which was a large metal, horn-shaped receptacle, into which the pilgrims passing by might cast their gifts.

Jesus, either standing or seated by the pillars of the courtyard, observed the pilgrim worshipers as they passed by the treasury. We know already that he was an unerring discerner of the inner motivations of men's actions. We seem to hear the echo of his earlier teaching, "Take heed that ye do not your alms before men, to be seen of them: otherwise ye have no reward of your Father which is in heaven." Did Jesus here see some ostentatiously parading their alms-giving? Did he observe how they waited until other pilgrims were present, and then threw in their coins so that the attention of every pilgrim would be turned upon them by the noise the coins made as they fell into the receptacle?

Jesus, as he observed the givers, discerned among them one, which prompted his calling of his disciples to see. A poor widow entered the courtyard of the treasury at a time when no others were at hand. Perhaps looking furtively about to make sure that none saw her, she opened her little money bag, took out two mites — all that the bag contained — and cast them quietly into the receptacle. So small and light of weight were the coins that not even a tinkle could be heard as they fell into the treasury. But Jesus read her inner disposition as well as her external act. To those who have purity of vision, outward acts reveal that which lies within the heart. Her posture, the grace of movement of her hand, the look upon her face — all revealed that she gave from love; she gave to God and sought not at all the esteem of men. She gave to God; and God " which seeth in secret " accepted her gift and blessed it.

This event and Jesus' evaluation of it rebuke much of our church money-giving. What is the disposition which motivates our giving at church services? We know that our hearts are open wide to the risen Jesus as we offer him our oblations.

63 THE TEMPLE

As he went out of the temple, one of his disciples saith unto him, Master, see what manner of stones and what buildings are here! And Jesus answering said unto him, Seest thou these great buildings? there shall not be left one stone upon another, that shall not be thrown down.

Mark 13: 1-2

This comment from one of Jesus' disciples seems to imply that he was not overfamiliar with the temple from many visits there. It is very likely that none of the chosen disciples were such zealous Jews as to have made the yearly pilgrimage to Jerusalem. To those accustomed to simple Galilean homes the massive stones of which the temple was constructed must have seemed most imposing. Moreover, this was the religious center of Judaism, and the size and magnificence of the temple architecture would be highly impressive to them.

But Jesus judged the temple not on the basis of its physical structure, its architecture. Only a few days before he had spoken out openly against the spirit which pervaded the temple buildings — a place of traffic and a den of thieves. A building — even this temple — which did not serve the purposes of God, and which would not be cleansed, must then be destroyed by God himself. Jesus' prediction was adequately fulfilled a generation later, when in 70 A.D. the Roman legions sacked the city and temple, leaving only a small portion of one wall intact. Jesus read accurately the signs of the times. Rome would in no way tolerate a growing Jewish nationalism; and Jesus knew, too, that God would not defend from the Romans a people who mocked God.

64 THE PARABLE OF THE FIG TREE

As he sat upon the mount of Olives over against the temple, Peter and James and John and Andrew asked him privately, Tell us, when shall these things be? and what shall be the sign when all these things shall be fulfilled?

And Jesus answering them began to say, . . . Now learn a parable of the fig tree; When her branch is yet tender, and putteth forth leaves, ye know that summer is near: So ye in like manner, when ye shall see these things come to pass, know that it is nigh, even at the doors. Verily I say unto you, that this generation shall not pass, till all these things be done. Heaven and earth shall pass away: but my words shall not pass away. But of that day and that hour knoweth no man, no, not the angels which are in heaven, neither the Son, but the Father. Take ye heed, watch and pray: for ye know not when the time is. For the Son of Man is as a man taking a far journey, who left his house, and gave authority to his servants, and to every man his work, and commanded the porter to watch. Watch ye therefore: for ye know not when the master of the house cometh, at even, or at midnight, or at the cock-crowing, or in the morning: lest coming suddenly he find you sleeping. And what I say unto you I say unto all, Watch.

Mark 13: 3-5a, 28-37

The greater part of the thirteenth chapter in Mark seems to be a primitive apocalyptical writing, which has been inserted into the record of events of this period in Jerusalem. We believe that it is a Jewish rather than a Christian writing.

Only these few verses from this chapter have been selected, because they seem to throw light upon the case of the fig tree. In Mark 11: 12-14 and 11: 20-26 we have the story of the cursing and the withering of a fig tree, because it did not bear fruit out of season — an action which fits ill into all that we know of Jesus' life and character. But here in this thirteenth chapter we are told that the fig tree is a parable of the signs of the times.

In Palestine the fig tree is the last tree in spring to bring forth its leaves. When it is in full leaf everybody knows that summer is near at hand. Jesus would apply this parable to the situation in Jerusalem at this time. A temple that will not be cleansed; a priesthood which does not serve God; a Pharisaism which is more concerned to perpetuate the traditions of men than to proclaim and obey the commandments of God; a rising Jewish nationalism daring to plot rebellion against the mighty Roman Empire: what are all these but clear, unequivocal signs that a day of divine judgment is at hand? To crown it all, when the servants of God are engaged in plotting and bringing to a quick fulfillment the death of Jesus, the Son of God, then God will act to judge and destroy.

Jesus' word to his disciples is clear and can be expressed in one decisive word — *watch*.

65 STRATEGY

After two days was the feast of the passover, and of unleavened bread: and the chief priests and the scribes sought how they might take him by craft, and put him to death. But they said, Not on the feast day, lest there be an uproar of the people.

Mark 14: 1-2

The enemies of Jesus dared not arrest him openly, in the presence of the pilgrim crowds. Yet they were determined to seize and kill Jesus during the time of the feast. The only problem was when and how. There must be no tumult, lest the Roman authorities step in.

During the feast *day* it would be impossible to carry out their plan, for then the streets of the city would be crowded with pilgrim supporters, and any arrest then would surely incite a riot. But on the *night* of the feast it would be quite another matter. (We must remember that with them the day began with sundown on Thursday.) During the evening and throughout the night the pilgrims would be either indoors eating the Passover supper, or later would be asleep. During that time Jesus could be arrested, be brought quietly and secretly before the council meeting in the palace of the high priest, and none of the pilgrims would know anything about it. Pilate would be holding his court very early Friday morning, and by the time the pilgrims were out upon the streets on Friday, Jesus would already be crucified. Such, as we shall see, was the plan shrewdly plotted and equally shrewdly carried out.

66 BETHANY

And being in Bethany in the house of Simon the leper, as he sat at meat, there came a woman having an alabaster box of ointment of spikenard very precious; and she brake the box, and poured it on his head. And there were some that had indignation within themselves, and said, Why was this waste of the ointment made? For it might have been sold for more than three hundred pence, and have been given to the poor. And they murmured against her.

And Jesus said, Let her alone; why trouble ye her? she hath wrought a good [beautiful] work on me. For ye have the poor with you always, and whensoever ye will ye may do them good: but me ye have not always. She hath done what she could: she is come aforehand to anoint my body to the burying. Verily I say unto you, Wheresoever this gospel shall be preached throughout the whole world, this also that she hath done shall be spoken of for a memorial of her.

Mark 14: 3-9

We naturally presume that Simon, the leper, may have been the leper whom Jesus had cured in Galilee, the story of which we find in Mark 1: 40-45. It was Simon's rare joy and privilege to be the last host of Jesus during his earthly life.

The Gospels nowhere reveal the identity of the woman of this story, and we must refrain from any attempt to search out her past. We sense simply that Jesus had done some great act of mercy to her or to somebody dear to her, and now she seeks to express her gratitude to Jesus.

The precious, costly perfume was contained in an equally expensive box of alabaster. A very few drops would have been sufficient to have anointed Jesus' head; but in her measureless gratitude she impulsively broke the alabaster box and poured the whole costly contents over his head. Some of us can remember having dropped and broken a small bottle of strong perfume in a room, and the utterly unbearable odor of it. The house of Simon must literally have reeked with the odor of the perfume, causing real discomfort to everybody in the room.

We can therefore quickly understand the open rebukes of the people there. " Why was this waste of the ointment made? " The woman could not help but hear their remarks. Has she done the wrong thing? The odor of the perfume certainly was overpowering, and what must it have been for Jesus especially? She had meant this act to be an expression of her gratitude and instead she had caused him discomfort. It was a waste.

Others might be indignant and censorious at the woman's act, but not Jesus. He counted the intention behind the act as the only true judgment of a human action. Nobody could have dealt more understandingly and courteously than Jesus. " Let her alone; why trouble ye her? " She hath wrought a good [beautiful] work on me." The Greek word may mean either " good " or " beautiful." Here it certainly should be translated as " beautiful." Whereas a good act is one that may be done in secret, a thing of beauty is meant to be seen by others.

How the woman's heart must have leaped with thankfulness for the understanding of Jesus. He had called her act a beautiful one. At once her heart was at peace. It mattered not a bit that these other people did not understand; Jesus did and that was sufficient.

Jesus has also a word for those who were indignant at the woman. " Ye have the poor with you always, and whensoever ye will ye may do them good." There will be ample opportunities in the future for doing good to the poor.

Jesus' next words would not have been understood by his hearers then, but they remembered them, and after his death realized their significance. The words again proclaim Jesus' imminent passion and death. ". . . me ye have not always." But only Jesus knew the full significance of those words. " She is come aforehand to anoint my body to the burying." Did Jesus foresee that he would be executed on the eve of a sabbath, necessitating a hurried burial with no time for proper anointing of his body? It could be that when he was taken down from the cross there still remained a faint odor of the spikenard.

Jesus' final word, that this beautiful act of the woman should be remembered throughout the whole world, wherever the gospel should be preached, has been fulfilled.

67 JUDAS ISCARIOT

And Judas Iscariot, one of the twelve, went unto the chief priests, to betray him unto them. And when they heard it, they were glad, and promised to give him money. And he sought how he might conveniently betray him.

Mark 14: 10-11

It is only in the Gospel according to John that any motivation is given for the treachery of Judas — that of avarice. We had better follow the much earlier and more trustworthy evidence of the first three Gospels, and refrain from attributing to Judas any motive that may not be true. It is so easy, as we all know from much experience, to misjudge motivations. The judgment of human hearts is the prerogative of God, not of men. He will judge rightly; we so often err.

A question of far greater importance for our understanding of the events which are quickly to happen to Jesus is that of *what* Judas betrayed. It certainly did not require Judas for the priests to discover that Jesus was accustomed to pass the nights during the feast in the Garden of Gethsemane. The secret police of the temple could easily have found that out for themselves.

It is Mark's account of the Gospel which alone affords us the clue to the answer of this important question. We remember that nobody except the twelve disciples of Jesus knows or even suspects that he is, or claims to be, the Messiah of God. Jesus at Caesarea Philippi had enjoined solemnly upon the twelve to keep this fact secret. This they had done, until Judas betrayed the secret to the high priest. Only so can we explain why, at the trial of Jesus before the Sanhedrin, the high priest could ask Jesus the decisive question, "Art thou the Messiah? " What Judas betrayed, we can thus know with a good degree of certainty; why Judas betrayed the secret, we do not know and must not presume to say.

We can readily understand the elation and joy of the high priests. They now had a charge against Jesus for which they could condemn him to death — the blasphemous claim to be the heavenly Messiah of God. Moreover, we presume, with Judas' connivance, they set a time and a place in which to arrest Jesus. What more perfect time to accomplish their plan than the night of the feast, when all the pilgrims would be in houses keeping the Passover, or asleep after it. The streets would be deserted and Jesus could be arrested and brought to the palace of the high priest with nobody aware of what had happened. And before the pilgrims would be on the streets the next morning, they would somehow contrive to have him delivered by Pilate to be crucified.

Moreover, Judas would prove useful in the actual arrest. Despite the full moon, it would take some moments to identify Jesus in the deep shadows of the olive trees. But if Judas would point out Jesus, then they could be sure to arrest him before he could make any attempt to escape.

68 PREPARING THE PASSOVER

The first day of unleavened bread, when they killed the passover, his disciples said unto him, Where wilt thou that we go and prepare that thou mayest eat the passover? And he sendeth forth two of his disciples, and saith unto them, Go ye into the city, and there shall meet you a man bearing a pitcher of water: follow him. And wheresoever he shall go in, say ye to the goodman of the house, The Master saith, Where is the guest-chamber, where I shall eat the passover with my disciples? And he will show you a large upper room furnished and prepared: there make ready for us.

And his disciples went forth, and came into the city, and found as he had said unto them: and they made ready the passover.

Mark 14: 12-16

Mark records that Jesus actually ate the Passover with his disciples, and in this both Luke and Matthew follow undeviatingly the same tradition. The later tradition given us by John relates a different record, in which Jesus was killed at the very hour that the lambs were being sacrificed in the temple for the Passover. Scholars are still divided as to the true chronology. If, as is quite possible, the Passover meal which Mark records was eaten in his own home, then Mark's evidence here must be taken as the true account.

We are not informed by Mark how Jesus had made the arrangements for the man with the water pitcher to identify the two disciples and lead them to the house where the Passover meal was to be eaten. There is no need that we should know. The secrecy with which Jesus planned the meeting place may be because Jesus was determined not to be secretly assassinated in the house, while eating the Passover meal. His death was not to be a murder, but a sacrifice, and made before the people openly.

69 FOOT-WASHING

Now before the feast of the passover, when Jesus knew that his hour was come that he should depart out of this world unto the Father, having loved his own which were in the world, he loved them unto the end. And supper being ended . . . Jesus . . . riseth from supper, and laid aside his garments; and took a towel, and girded himself. After that he poureth water into a basin, and began to wash the disciples' feet, and to wipe them with the towel wherewith he was girded.

Then cometh he to Simon Peter: and Peter saith unto him, Master, dost thou wash my feet? Jesus answered and said unto him, What I do thou knowest not now; but thou shalt know hereafter. Peter saith unto him, Thou shalt never wash my feet. Jesus answered him, If I wash thee not, thou hast no part with me. Simon Peter saith unto him, Master, not my feet only, but also my hands and my head. Jesus saith to him, He that is washed needeth not save to wash his feet, but is clean every whit. . . .

So after he had washed their feet, and had taken his garments, and was set down again, he said unto them, Know ye what I have done to you? Ye call me Master and Messiah: and ye say well; for so I am. If I then, your Messiah and Master, have washed your feet; ye also ought to wash one another's feet. For I have given you an example, that ye should do as I have done to you.

John 13: 1-15

Only John records this event, and of its historical truth we can have no doubt. Whether this meal was held on Thursday evening, or some evening earlier, we cannot be sure, since John does not record at all the Last Supper.

The duty of washing the feet of guests was assigned to a house slave. Never was such a function performed by a superior. To the amazement of the disciples, Jesus after supper laid aside his outer garment, took a towel, and girded himself with it, poured water into a basin, and began to wash the feet of the disciples, and to wipe them with the towel with which he was girded. The Messiah of God kneeling at the feet of twelve disciples, performing the role of a humble house slave! We can at once understand Peter's impulsive protest at this unseemly action of Jesus. It was just not fitting for him to be doing the work of a common household slave. " Master, dost *thou* wash *my* feet? "

This is not the first time that Jesus had to correct Peter, but we do marvel at the loving patience of Jesus towards him. Any other teacher would long ago have given up Peter as hopeless. With no bending, and with no argument, Jesus quietly tells Peter, "What I do thou knowest not now; but thou shalt know hereafter." How often we, too, fail to grasp the significance of an act at the time it is done; only after the passage of time are we awakened to its import.

Peter could not understand it yet. He again impulsively blurts out, "Thou shalt never wash my feet." A second time Jesus has firmly but lovingly to correct Peter. "If I wash thee not, thou hast no part with me." These words reached Peter's heart, as the former words had failed to reach or win his obedience. Not to have any part with Jesus was more than Peter could accept.

Was it that Peter felt himself unworthy of accepting this act at the hands of Jesus, that he then blurts out, "Master, not my feet only, but also my hands and my head"? Or is it perhaps Peter's subtle determination to divert Jesus from this unseemly slave act, and have it done in a way chosen by Peter himself? How often we tell God how and when he should act in his dealings with us, and refuse to accept his appointed ways of salvation. Jesus will not compromise or change.

Only when Jesus had washed and wiped the feet of all the disciples did he then turn to his silent, staring friends, look into their wondering eyes, and interpret the meaning of this strange, unprecedented action. "If I then, your Messiah and Master, have washed your feet; ye also ought to wash one another's feet. For I have given you an example, that ye should do as I have done to you." We wonder if some of them remembered an occasion which had happened just as they had left Galilee a short while ago, when by the way they had disputed which of them should be the greatest.

70 PROPHECY OF BETRAYAL

In the evening he cometh with the twelve. And as they sat and did eat, Jesus said, Verily I say unto you, One of you which eateth with me shall betray me. And they began to be sorrowful, and to say unto him one by one, Is it I? and another said, Is it I? And he answered and said unto them, It is one of the twelve, that dippeth with me in the dish. The Son of Man indeed goeth, as it is written of him: but woe to that man by whom the Son of Man is betrayed! good were it for that man if he had never been born.

Mark 14: 17-21

". . . One of you which eateth with me shall betray me." It is noteworthy, as revealing the character of each of the twelve, that none said, "Is it *he?*" The doubt in each man's heart was first of all of himself. "I, I betray him? It cannot be; yet perhaps it may be I."

Here again we have every good reason to trust the account given us by Mark, all the more so when we compare it with that given us by John and Matthew. John writes:

"Verily, verily, I say unto you, that one of you shall betray me. Then the disciples looked one on another, doubting of whom he spake. Now there was leaning on Jesus' bosom one of his disciples, whom Jesus loved. Simon Peter therefore beckoned to him, that he should ask who it should be of whom he spake. He then lying on Jesus' breast saith unto him, Master, who is it? Jesus answered, He it is, to whom I shall give a sop, when I have dipped it. And when he had dipped the sop, he gave it to Judas Iscariot, the son of Simon. . . . He then having received the sop went immediately out: and it was night."

Psychologically it is most difficult to believe that Peter and the beloved disciple, once they have learned who was the betrayer, would quietly have allowed him to go out to fulfill his act of betrayal. Such nonchalance in no way fits into the picture we have of impetuous Peter.

Matthew records that Judas himself asks, "Is it I?" Then

Jesus immediately replies unto him before them all, "Thou hast said," thus revealing to all the disciples who the betrayer was. And there is no sequel to the momentous disclosure.

Mark's account has about it the ring of psychological truth. Jesus is courteous even to his betrayer. Perhaps his prophecy was directed to the heart of Judas, to carry a last appeal to him to repent. We cannot think of Jesus as revealing the heart and purpose of Judas to his fellow disciples.

If Mark's record be the true one, then Judas would, in the absence of any evidence to the contrary, have been present throughout the Last Supper. Only when they left the house to go outside of the city to the Garden of Gethsemane would Judas have lingered behind as the band turned the corner of one of the darkened streets, and then gone his own way to the palace of the high priest.

Let us who read of the betrayal of Jesus by Judas be imitators of Jesus' own courtesy towards him. We remember that on another occasion Jesus told a group of Pharisees that only the man who was without sin might first cast a stone at a sinful woman. None of us dares cast a stone at Judas. We may even hope that there is room in the heart of God for forgiveness of Judas. Let our faith be great enough to grasp even that, to us, impossible action.

71 BREAD – BODY; WINE – BLOOD

And as they did eat, Jesus took bread, and blessed, and brake it, and gave to them, and said, Take, eat: this is my body.

And he took the cup, and when he had given thanks, he gave it to them: and they all drank of it. And he said unto them, This is my blood of the new testament, which is shed for many. Verily I say unto you, I will drink no more of the fruit of the vine, until that day that I drink it new in the kingdom of God.

Mark 14: 22-25

This is Jesus' last parable, a parable uttered not in words, but by an act. Teaching through words was now inadequate

Late on Thursday night Jesus and his disciples left the home of John Mark, to go out into the darkened, deserted streets of Jerusalem on their way out of the city to the Garden of Gethsemane. As they walk with Jesus he gives them still another hard word. "All ye shall be offended because of me this night. . . . But after I am risen, I will go before you into Galilee."

Already that evening he had declared unto them that one of them would this same night betray him. Now Jesus tells them *all* that *all* of them will abandon him. Jesus knew the innermost heart of each of his disciples with perfect knowledge.

Again Peter would refute Jesus. Much must happen to impulsive, impetuous Peter before he will become truly humble, docile, obedient. Each of us can take heart from the example of Peter. If Jesus would not abandon him, despite all his many failures, we can trust him never to forsake us, no matter how often we may fail him.

Peter's words really are a boast, "Although all shall be offended, yet will not I." And Peter really believed his own words, not knowing himself. But there is no scolding and no lecturing in Jesus' reply to Peter, but only the quiet, sad proclaiming of a truth, which future events will entirely substantiate. ". . . this day, even in this night, before the cock crow, thou shalt deny me thrice." Jesus singles out Peter for an especial offense, such as will not be shared by the other disciples. And here again Peter contradicts Jesus. "If I should die with thee, I will not deny thee in any wise." Misled by Peter, the ten join in a common protest against Jesus' prophecy concerning them. How little any of the eleven knew their own hearts and wills. Only men truly and deeply humbled and transformed by the resurrection would have dared to record this event concerning themselves.

The " cock crow " is the name given to one of the watches of the night, when the Roman soldiers on guard duty changed their watch. We presume it was so named because it came just before early dawn, a time when the roosters began to crow. Before dawn on this Friday, Peter will have disowned Jesus thrice.

It well may have been that it was while they were walking through the quiet, deserted, darkened streets of Jerusalem that Judas would lag behind, perhaps stooping as if to tie a sandal thong. Then, as the band turned a corner, he went in the other direction and on to the palace of the high priest to fulfill his promise of betrayal. The eleven disciples may not even have noticed his departure in the darkness. It is unlikely however that Judas' act escaped the watchful eyes of Jesus. While Judas walked with swift feet to complete his infamous act, we think of Jesus interceding for him and offering to him his full, free forgiveness.

In this passage we also have the first prediction from Jesus' own lips that it would be in *Galilee* that he would appear to the disciples after his resurrection from the dead. It is a prediction which we shall need to remember when we come to the stories of the resurrection.

73 GETHSEMANE

They came to a place which was named Gethsemane: and he saith to his disciples, Sit ye here, while I shall pray. And he taketh with him Peter and James and John, and began to be sore amazed, and to be very heavy; and saith unto them, My soul is exceeding sorrowful unto death: tarry ye here, and watch.

And he went forward a little, and fell on the ground, and prayed that, if it were possible, the hour might pass from him. And he said, Abba, Father, all things are possible unto thee; take away this cup from me: nevertheless not what I will, but what thou wilt.

And he cometh, and findeth them sleeping, and saith unto Peter, Simon, sleepest thou? couldest not thou watch one hour? Watch ye and pray, lest ye enter into temptation. The spirit truly is ready, but the flesh is weak. And again he went away, and prayed, and spake the same words.

And when he returned, he found them asleep again, (for their eyes were heavy,) neither wist they what to answer him. And he cometh the third time, and saith unto them, Sleep on now, and take your rest: it is enough,

the hour is come; behold, the Son of man is betrayed into the hands of
sinners. Rise up, let us go; lo, he that betrayeth me is at hand.

Mark 14: 32-42

The Garden of Gethsemane was the place where Jesus and
his disciples were accustomed to pass the nights during the feast.
This was the place and this was the time for sleep; and that is
what they did. Even though Jesus bade eight of the disciples
to sit, while he prayed, they soon fell asleep.

Then taking Peter, James, and John apart from the eight
disciples, Jesus asked them to watch while he prayed. One
hour — sixty long, consecutive minutes — of agonized waiting
for Judas to complete his act of betrayal. For it would take
Judas not more than the sixty minutes to go to the palace, join
the band who were to arrest Jesus, and then lead them to
Gethsemane. Close by the garden lay the road leading to
Galilee. Merely by taking that road during this hour, Jesus
could be safe. Once these sixty minutes were ended, there
would no longer be any such opportunity of escape.

Of his chosen twelve friends, one was at that very moment
bringing those who were to arrest him; before dawn another
would deny him with a curse; and every one of them would
this night abandon him. All the religious leaders were against
him. That which long ago in the wilderness temptations had
been intimated to him had now come to pass. The kingdom of
God would not and could not come by his preaching, nor by
his life. Only by his death could the Kingdom come. His death
was to be a sacrifice.

Too often Jesus had seen crucified figures as he traversed the
roads of Palestine, for it was customary for the Romans to hold
executions publicly on the main roads, that travelers passing by
might be warned of the consequences of civil disobedience and
crime. Being himself a Jew, Jesus knew that the manner of his
death would be crucifixion. His true and full humanity naturally
shrank from the ordeal that lay ahead of him. Jesus has de-

scribed his agony for us in the imagery of a cup offered to him from the hand of God, that he should drink it to the dregs. It is significant that Jesus interprets the cup as being offered by God, not by the hands of sinful men. Jesus has given us the words of the prayer that he prayed. "Abba, Father, all things are possible unto thee; take away this cup from me: nevertheless not what I will, but what thou wilt."

He who had taught his disciples to pray " Thy will be done " now himself prays in like fashion. The word " nevertheless " means far more than resignation; it signifies the glad, instantaneous identification of his will with that of God; and in it is involved the total and full surrender of his will to God. Here in this prayer Jesus accepts crucifixion, as the way appointed of God for the coming of the Kingdom.

Thrice during this one hour Jesus came to the three sleeping disciples, those whom he had bidden to watch. Let us be very sure that Jesus came to them not to get help and strength and companionship. It is inconceivable to think of him as turning for help to Peter, who before the dawn will have denied that he even knows Jesus; or to James and John, who, with Peter, will have fled north to Galilee, abandoning him. Jesus knew where to turn for sure strength and true companionship – to God in prayer. Rather, Jesus went thrice to them to give to them his own alert watchfulness and prayerfulness. What man is this, who in the very heart of his own agony can so forget himself, and be concerned with his three sleeping disciples? Jesus knew the terrible and dangerous temptations that beset them this very night, and knew that they could be met victoriously only by the power of prayer. Jesus' faith is not in these three sleepy disciples, but in God. He trusted that God could save Peter, James, and John in spite of themselves.

It was Jesus, and not the disciples, who discerned the band approaching to arrest him. From now on Jesus will be literally *alone*. The salvation which he will earn for us will in no part be shared in by any of the disciples. They will not figure again in the gospel story until after the resurrection, and then as witnesses to that mighty event.

The hour is come. That hour, envisioned as early as the time of the wilderness temptations, accepted fully and clearly in anticipation at the Transfiguration, and which he had just drunk from the cup offered him by God in Gethsemane — that hour has at last come. The crucifixion is now irrevocable. It remains only to carry it out.

Strange paradox — the Son of God handed over into the hands of sinful men, religious leaders of the people of God. "He came unto his own people, and they received him not." Sincerely, but horribly mistaken, they think they serve God by putting this Jesus to death.

74 BETRAYAL CONSUMMATED

Immediately, while he yet spake, cometh Judas, one of the twelve, and with him a great multitude with swords and staves, from the chief priests and the scribes and the elders. And he that betrayed him had given them a token, saying, Whomsoever I shall kiss, that same is he; take him, and lead him away safely. And as soon as he was come, he goeth straightway to him, and saith, Master, Master; and kissed him.

And Jesus said unto him, Friend, wherefore art thou come?

And they laid their hands on him, and took him. And one of them that stood by drew a sword, and smote a servant of the high priest, and cut off his ear. And Jesus answered and said unto them, Are ye come out, as against a thief, with swords and with staves to take me? I was daily with you in the temple teaching, and ye took me not. . . .

And they all forsook him, and fled. And there followed him a certain young man, having a linen cloth cast about his naked body; and the young men laid hold on him: and he left the linen cloth, and fled from them naked.

Mark 14: 43-45; Matthew 26: 50; Mark 14: 46-52

That which Jesus had foretold is fulfilled. One of the twelve — Judas — betrays him with a kiss. It is only Matthew here who gives us a most significant insight into this event. None of the other writers have grasped it. We should have expected the reaction of Jesus to have been expressed in some such words as " traitor," " you," " Judas." Instead, we hear that utterly unexpected word "Friend." Not even this perfidious act of treachery could terminate Jesus' loving and redemptive friendship for Judas.

This is the last recorded word that Jesus spake during his earthly life to any disciple; and it is a word of love and spoken to one who betrayed him. We believe that in that one word Jesus offered to Judas full, free, unconditional forgiveness from God, forever and forever. We wonder what response came from the heart of Judas as he heard that word "Friend."

We cannot for a moment believe that it is by sheer accident that Matthew records this word of Jesus. We remember that in the parable of the vineyard workers that same word " Friend " also appears, again in a setting where it is the last word we should have expected.

Jesus, who had taught men " not to resist evil," now himself does not resist. He does not seek to flee. Quietly and calmly, and as master even of this situation, he speaks his words to those who have just arrested him. "Are ye come out, as against a thief, with swords and staves, to take me? I was daily with you in the temple teaching, and ye took me not."

"And they all forsook him, and fled." Again Jesus' prophecy concerning the disciples is fulfilled. We presume that they fled along the road to Galilee, in fear for their lives. We shall not again see anything of them, excepting in one short episode involving Peter, until the resurrection morning on the shore of the Lake of Galilee. For them this was the *end*. It was all a great hoax and delusion. Jesus was an impostor. Had he truly been the Messiah of God, this could not have happened. There was nothing now but to take due concern for their own safety.

" There followed him a certain young man, having a linen cloth cast about his naked body." These words may be John Mark's unobtrusive witness to being himself an eyewitness of

these events. If the Last Supper had taken place in his own
home, it could well have been that John Mark, the young lad,
had with curiosity been moved impulsively to follow Jesus and
the disciples, when they left his home, and followed them to the
Garden of Gethsemane. There not being time to dress fully,
he had simply cast about his naked body a sheet from his bed.
The young man certainly cannot be a Galilean pilgrim; for
pilgrims do not use bed sheets.

75 DENIAL BY PETER

They led Jesus away to the high priest: and with him were assembled
all the chief priests and the elders and the scribes. And Peter followed
him afar off, even into the palace of the high priest: and he sat with the
servants, and warmed himself at the fire. . . .

And as Peter was beneath in the palace, there cometh one of the maids
of the high priest: and when she saw Peter warming himself, she looked
upon him, and said, And thou also wast with Jesus of Nazareth. But he
denied, saying, I know not, neither understand I what thou sayest. And
he went out into the porch; and the cock crew. And a maid saw him again,
and began to say to them that stood by, This is one of them. And he
denied it again. And a little after, they that stood by said again to Peter,
Surely thou art one of them: for thou art a Galilean, and thy speech
agreeth thereto. But he began to curse and to swear, saying, I know not
this man of whom ye speak.

And the second time the cock crew. And Peter called to mind the
word that Jesus said unto him, Before the cock crow twice, thou shalt
deny me thrice. And when he thought thereon, he wept.

                              Mark 14: 53-54, 66-72. Alt. by Matthew.

Peter had boasted that even though all should be offended
against Jesus, yet he would not. It was Peter alone who dared to
follow from afar the party which had arrested Jesus in Gethsemane. He even dared to enter into the courtyard of the priestly
palace. But even in the last darkness of the passing night Peter
could not conceal the fact that he did not belong there. Even
a servant girl could spot him as being a Galilean peasant. Not
only his dress, but also his speech betrayed him as a stranger.

Thrice challenged, thrice Peter denied even knowing Jesus, the last time with impulsive cursing and swearing.

Dawn was coming, and the first rooster crowed to herald the coming day. And suddenly Peter remembered the words of Jesus, " Before the cock crow thou shalt deny me thrice." And the rough, impetuous Peter wept.

The fact that the Gospels in no wise try to paint the disciples as perfect men, but instead frankly and impartially record their many failures and weaknesses speaks much for the trustworthiness of the gospel traditions. Only Peter could have told this story about himself, and we can well believe that he recounted it humbly and penitently.

We presume that Peter rejoined the other ten disciples on the road to Galilee, and together they made the journey back to the lake, dejected, brokenhearted, fearful men. It was the end of their dreams.

76 CONDEMNATION BY THE COUNCIL

The chief priests and all the council sought for witness against Jesus to put him to death; and found none. For many bare false witness against him, but their witness agreed not together. And there arose certain, and bare false witness against him, saying, We heard him say, I will destroy this temple that is made with hands, and within three days I will build another made without hands. But neither so did their witness agree together.

And the high priest stood up in the midst, and asked Jesus, saying, Answerest thou nothing? what is it which these witness against thee? But he held his peace, and answered nothing. Again the high priest asked him, and said unto him, Art thou the Messiah, the Son of the Blessed?

And Jesus said, I am: and ye shall see the Son of Man sitting on the right hand of the Power, and coming in the clouds of heaven.

Then the high priest rent his clothes, and saith, What need we any further witnesses? Ye have heard the blasphemy: what think ye? And they all condemned him to be guilty of death. And some began to spit on him, and to cover his face, and to buffet him, and to say unto him, Prophesy: and the servants did strike him with the palms of their hands.

Mark 14: 55-65

The fact that here, in the small hours of early dawn, the whole council was ready assembled is evidence of the shrewdly planned plot of the high priest. It may have been that part of his bargain with Judas was that Judas should bear witness against Jesus before the council. But Judas is not here. Had Jesus' last word to him — "Friend" — so reached his heart, that he could not carry through the whole of his agreement, but had instead committed suicide? We do not know; but it is evident that the last-minute attempts to secure witnesses to condemn Jesus were not going well. Without two witnesses in agreement, no condemnation could be secured from the council.

Finally the high priest himself asked of Jesus, "Art thou the Messiah, the Son of the Blessed?" How did he know the secret of Jesus being the Messiah, when only the twelve knew it? It seems almost conclusive then to believe that Judas had betrayed to the high priest Jesus' claim to be the Messiah.

Jesus answered, "I am; and ye shall see the Son of Man sitting on the right hand of the Power, and coming in the clouds of heaven." Both Jesus and the high priest follow the strict Jewish custom of not using the term God, but instead use synonyms — "the Blessed," "the Power."

With Jesus' own admission of being the Messiah, there was no longer need of the evidence of witnesses to condemn him. The whole court were the witnesses of his confession, which according to Jewish law constituted blasphemy. The penalty for blasphemy was death. There remained now only to scheme the means by which they might secure from Pilate his condemnation of this Jesus to death. While they planned that procedure, Jesus was made the sport of the servants. No more insulting indignity can be offered to an Oriental than to spit upon him. The picture here is a strange paradox — Jesus, the Son of God, blindfolded, buffeted, spit upon by the servants of the high priest of God.

77 BROUGHT TO PILATE

Straightway in the morning the chief priests held a consultation with the elders and scribes and the whole council, and bound Jesus, and carried him away, and delivered him to Pilate. And Pilate asked him, Art thou the King of the Jews? And he answering said unto him, Thou sayest it.

And the chief priests accused him of many things: but he answered nothing. And Pilate asked him again, saying, Answerest thou nothing? behold how many things they witness against thee. But Jesus yet answered nothing; so that Pilate marvelled.

Now at that feast he released unto them one prisoner, whomsoever they desired. And there was one named Barabbas, which lay bound with them that had made insurrection with him, who had committed murder in the insurrection.

And the multitude crying aloud began to desire him to do as he had ever done unto them. But Pilate answered them, saying, Will ye that I release unto you the King of the Jews? For he knew that the chief priests had delivered him for envy. But the chief priests moved the people, that he should rather release Barabbas unto them. And Pilate answered and said again unto them, What will ye then that I shall do unto him whom ye call the King of the Jews? And they cried out again, Crucify him. Then Pilate said unto them, Why, what evil hath he done? And they cried out the more exceedingly, Crucify him.

And so Pilate, willing to content the people, released Barabbas unto them, and delivered Jesus, when he had scourged him, to be crucified.

Mark 15: 1-15

The normal residence of Pontius Pilate was not at Jerusalem, but at Caesarea. On the occasion of the annual great feasts of the Jews, when Jewish patriotism ran high, there was serious danger of revolts and riots. At such times, therefore, Pilate was accustomed to come to Jerusalem with military reinforcements for the Roman garrison stationed there, in order to be prepared for any emergencies.

Moreover, it was customary to hold over for his annual visits the more difficult court cases, that he himself might give judgment upon them. Once each year, at the feast of the Passover, Pilate granted amnesty to one political prisoner, whom the Jewish populace might select. It so happened that on this particular year there lay in prison at Jerusalem one Barabbas, a Jewish patriot who had committed murder in the insurrection which he had led.

Weeks before Pilate's coming to Jerusalem there would be posted on the walls of the city streets (the equivalent of our public bulletin boards) a list of the cases which Pilate would hear, and the hours at which the cases would come before him. We can well believe that the case of Barabbas would have been well publicized, and that a large following of his sympathizers would plan to be on hand for his trial, eager to secure for him Pilate's grant of amnesty.

The case of Jesus, however, could not possibly have been posted, for only during the preceding night had he been arrested. None of the Galilean pilgrims knew anything about his arrest or condemnation, nor that he had been brought early on Friday morning before Pilate. None of the Galileans would be interested during the feast to climb the hill to Pilate's palace to hear the case of Barabbas, whom they did not know. Thus Jesus would have not even one friend in court, when his case was heard, but only his enemies. The followers of Barabbas would have no concern for his fate.

According to the tradition given us by Mark, Jesus was actually crucified at nine o'clock in the morning, and such an hour fits in very well with the occasion. Pilate would want to finish up the court cases as early in the morning as possible, in order that he might then be free to deal with any incipient riots during the feast day. We can think then of the trial as taking place early in the morning, even as early as six o'clock. The court was held out in the open street in front of the Praetorium, so that all concerned might attend. Pilate would have his throne of judgment carried out and placed before the gates of the palace. Then court would open.

Pilate knew from years of experience the bitter animosity between the people and the high priests. Invariably they were on opposite sides of any question. Pilate suspected therefore that the case of Jesus would be another one in which the people and the high priests would be on opposite sides. But to his wonderment he found on this occasion that the priests and the people were of one mind.

The followers of Barabbas would cry out for Pilate's release of their hero, and in that cry the high priests would gladly and wholeheartedly join. If Barabbas were freed, that meant the impossibility of release for Jesus. And when Pilate sought to divert the attention of the multitude to Jesus, they cried out spontaneously, "Crucify him." They cared not at all what might happen to Jesus, so long as Barabbas was freed. We err greatly when we believe that the crowd who cry out here "Crucify him" are the same crowd that welcomed Jesus on his entrance into Jerusalem with ovations and Hosannas. That crowd was composed of Galilean pilgrims; this is composed entirely of the supporters of Barabbas and the enemies of Jesus.

This was the great feast day. Better to release Barabbas unto the crowd than face this early in the day a popular riot. Best, too, to sacrifice this obscure Galilean and so appease the temple priests. So Pilate released Barabbas to his followers and handed over Jesus, after scourging, to the soldiers to crucify.

78 MOCKING

And the soldiers led him away into the hall, called Praetorium; and they called together the whole band. And they clothed him with purple, and platted a crown of thorns, and put it about his head, and began to salute him, Hail, King of the Jews! And they smote him on the head with a reed, and did spit upon him, and bowing their knees worshipped him. And when they had mocked him, they took off the purple from him, and put his own clothes on him, and led him out to crucify him.

Mark 15: 16-20

Here is evidence that the court trial was held in the street, for now the soldiers led Jesus away into the Praetorium. It would be desirable to despatch with as much haste as possible the three executions, as this was the great day of the feast, and before long the streets of Jerusalem would be thronged with pilgrims. While a detachment of the soldiers were preparing the details of the crucifixion, the rest of the band made sport of Jesus, and we presume also of the two others who were to be executed with him. The rough, hardened Roman soldiers had their brutal play with Jesus. So this one claimed to be King of the Jews! Well, then, they would treat him as a king. Dressing him up in an old purple robe, and placing a crown of thorns none too gently upon his head, they mocked him as a king. And Jesus was a king — God's King — and they knew it not. And we can know that Jesus forgave them, for they knew not what they did.

79 CRUCIFIXION

And they compel one Simon, a Cyrenian, who passed by, coming out of the country, the father of Alexander and Rufus, to bear his cross. And they bring him unto the place Golgotha, which is, being interpreted, The place of a skull.

And they gave him to drink wine mingled with myrrh: but he received it not. And when they had crucified him, they parted his garments, casting lots upon them, what every man should take. And it was the third hour, and they crucified him. And the superscription of his accusation was written over, THE KING OF THE JEWS.

And with him they crucify two thieves; the one on his right hand, and the other on his left. . . . And they that passed by railed on him, wagging their heads, and saying, Ah, thou that destroyest the temple, and buildest it in three days, save thyself, and come down from the cross. Likewise also the chief priests mocking said among themselves with the scribes, He saved others; himself he cannot save. Let Messiah the King of Israel descend now from the cross, that we may see and believe. And they that were crucified with him reviled him.

Mark 15: 21-32

It was customary for the Romans to carry out the executions of criminals beside the main roads, and to make a public exhibition of the victims. Golgotha was outside the city of Jerusalem on the main road.

The one touch of mercy shown towards the victims to be crucified was to offer them an anesthetic to deaden the pain — wine mingled with myrrh. The gospel tradition records that Jesus refused this alleviation of the pain which faced him. At the Last Supper he had said that he would drink no more of the fruit of the vine until that day when he would drink it new in the kingdom of God. He would meet death with all his senses clear and alert. He would drink to the dregs the cup which God had placed in his hands.

Mark explicitly states that it was at the third hour (nine o'clock in the morning) that Jesus was crucified. According to the tradition of John, the trial of Jesus before Pilate was still taking place at noon — a tradition which in no way fits into the situation. It is most unlikely that Pilate would provoke the Jews by leading three victims for crucifixion through the crowded streets of Jerusalem at high noon. Under Mark's timing, Jesus would have been led out of the city as early as eight o'clock on Friday morning, at a time before the pilgrim crowds would throng the streets. Jesus would have been actually upon his cross by the time that any of the Galilean pilgrims heard of it. Over Jesus' head, nailed to the cross, was the placard stating the crime for which he was being put to death — "The King of the Jews." He was truly the King of the Jews — given them by God himself — but they knew it not.

It is noteworthy that none of the Gospels give us any of the details of the crucifixion. We today had best follow the reverent reticence of the gospel writers, and seek not to harry our imaginations with the terrible details of the six hours of agony upon the cross. Pity on our part for Jesus is out of place; rather it is he who pities us, our sin, and our blindness.

In the jibes and mocking of the passers-by, the chief priests, and the fellow victims, we are given the judgment of the world upon Jesus — God's King. They counted this ignominious death of Jesus as the end, as his failure. To every human eye it looked like stark and tragic defeat, the bringing to nought of all that Jesus had taught and lived. This was proof conclusive that God himself had rejected Jesus. Here at the end, as at the beginning of his ministry, Jesus is besieged by temptations. " Let Messiah, the King of Israel, descend now from the cross, that we may see and believe." What is that but a repetition of the satanic temptation in the wilderness to use a miracle to amaze people into the kingdom of God? " He saved others; himself he cannot save." What is that but the satanic temptation that being Messiah, he will be protected by the angels against all hurt?

80 DEATH

When the sixth hour was come, there was darkness over the whole land until the ninth hour. And at the ninth hour Jesus cried with a loud voice, saying, Eli, Eli, lama sabachthani? which is, being interpreted, My God, my God, why hast thou forsaken me?

And some of them that stood by, when they heard it, said, This man calleth for Elias. And straightway one of them ran, and took a sponge, and filled it with vinegar, and put it on a reed, and gave him to drink. The rest said, Let be, let us see whether Elias will come to save him.

And Jesus cried with a loud voice, and gave up the ghost. And the veil of the temple was rent in twain from the top to the bottom. And when the centurion, which stood over against him, saw that he so cried out, and gave up the ghost, he said, Truly this man was a Son of God.

There were also women looking on afar off: among whom was Mary Magdalene, and Mary the mother of James the less and of Joses, and Salome; (who also, when he was in Galilee, followed him, and ministered unto him;) and many other women which came up with him into Jerusalem.

                                        Mark 15: 33-41. Alt. by Matthew

According to this, our earliest written gospel tradition, corroborated by Matthew, Jesus during the long six hours upon the cross uttered two cries only at the very end — at three o'clock. It was customary for the crucified victims to rage and curse in their agony. The silence of Jesus upon the cross, as also his strange silences at his two trials when he refused to open his lips to defend himself, made a deep impression upon the earliest Christians. In Acts 8: 32 the early Christians interpreted Jesus' silence as the fulfillment of the ancient prophecy of Isaiah:

> He was led as a sheep to the slaughter; and like a lamb
> dumb before his shearer, so opened he not his mouth.

The two cries at the end were that terrible cry of dereliction, so terrible that only on the basis that it was true did the church preserve it — " Elí, Elí, lama sabachthani "; and then at the very end an inarticulate cry as he dies.

We have used the text of Matthew here, even though it is the harder reading; but we believe that the original text of Mark must have read likewise. The first two words are in the Hebrew tongue, and the last two words in Aramaic, the language spoken by Jesus. The cry, half in Hebrew and half in Aramaic, is required in order to understand the bewilderment and misinterpretation of the crowds who heard it. Jesus is reported to have cried the words with a loud voice, and therefore it is hard to understand why they were not understood. True, nobody expected to hear the name of God (El) cried from the cross, for Jews so rigidly reverenced the name of God that they pronounced it only in reading from and quoting the Scriptures. Yet they would certainly be able to recognize the name for God when they heard it. The Aramaic word for God — Éloi — to our ears does not at all sound like Elíya (Elijah), whom they mistakenly believed him to be calling to his aid, like a sort of patron saint of trouble. Commonly the Jews pronounced Éli with the accent upon the first syllable. Then it meant " My *God*." But then we are still unable to understand why they could have confused it with Elíya, which is accented on the second syllable. But if Jesus gave a pronunciation never before heard, placing

the accent on the suffix " Elí," then it would sound very much
like Elíya, and we can at once understand that the people
thought him to be calling upon Elijah. In support of this interpretation, we have the additional evidence from the translator
of Dante, who writes in his Purgatorio xxiii 73 ff:

> For that desire leads us to the Tree,
> Which led Christ *joyfully* to cry Elí,
> What time he freed us with his precious blood ...

where Elí rhymes with Tree, and the cry is associated with
" joy."

When Jesus uttered the cry at three o'clock, the sense of
being abandoned by God was over and finished. Now he can
joyfully and peacefully cry out, " *My* God, *My* God." *That*
cry is one filled with joy at having once more the sense of God's
presence, and the peace of knowing that he had perfectly fulfilled God's will. The abandonment by God had been endured
in the silence of the six long hours. Now Jesus had perfect joy
and peace. He had not failed God. He had perfectly revealed
God's heart, God's mighty, unbending love.

Our gospel traditions record that nature itself reacted in
sympathy with this great event — in the darkness which spread
over the scene from noon until three o'clock, as also in the
earthquake which rent the veil of the temple. Even nature
could not tolerate this outrage against the Son of God.

Here too we have our only indication in the Gospels that
Jesus during his ministry was cared for by a group of women
of Galilee. Knowing that Jesus had two brothers named James
and Joses, we may presume that the Mary so described is Jesus'
mother. But these stood afar off.

Even the hardened centurion had been deeply impressed by
the way in which Jesus had died. Never before had he seen a
crucified victim die in this fashion. But we are not to read

more into his words than the simple evaluation that Jesus had shown himself worthy to be *a* son of God. It is utterly impossible that the centurion by his words meant that Jesus was *the* Son of God.

81 BURIAL

And now when even was come, because it was the preparation, that is, the day before the sabbath, Joseph of Arimathea, an honourable counsellor, which also waited for the kingdom of God, came, and went in boldly unto Pilate, and craved the body of Jesus.

And Pilate marvelled if he were already dead: and calling unto him the centurion, he asked him whether he had been any while dead.

And when he knew it of the centurion, he gave the body to Joseph. And he bought fine linen, and took him down, and wrapped him in the linen, and laid him in a sepulchre which was hewn out of a rock, and rolled a stone unto the door of the sepulchre. And Mary Magdalene and Mary the mother of Joses beheld where he was laid.

Mark 15: 42-47

If any of the friends or disciples of Jesus had been present at the crucifixion, we should have expected them to have undertaken the duty of burying Jesus. The tradition given us by Mark clearly indicates that none was there, except the two Marys, who looked on from afar. Thus we have here additional support for our belief that the disciples of Jesus had fled north to Galilee, in fear for their lives.

Instead we find a total stranger, Joseph of Arimathea, undertaking the task of giving hurried burial to the body of Jesus. Was it simply that Joseph had been deeply impressed by the manner of Jesus' death — his silence and meekness? It was not fitting that one who could so die should be cast into the common grave for criminals. His own burial tomb was near by, and he volunteered to give decent burial to Jesus.

The Jewish sabbath would begin at sundown. Jesus had died at the ninth hour (three o'clock). Little time remained in which to make the trip from Golgotha to Pilate's palace, have Pilate make due inquiry from the centurion of Jesus' death, buy supplies of linen, and make the return journey to Golgotha, and bury Jesus in the sepulchre. There was thus no time carefully to anoint the body of Jesus; but we know that Jesus had counted the anointing of the woman at Bethany his burial anointing. And from his head perhaps there would still come a faint odor of the spikenard.

PART SEVEN

GOD'S MIGHTY ACT

82 THE WOMEN AT THE TOMB

When the sabbath was past, Mary Magdalene, and Mary the mother of James, and Salome, had bought sweet spices, that they might come and anoint him. And very early in the morning the first day of the week, they came unto the sepulchre at the rising of the sun. And they said among themselves, Who shall roll us away the stone from the door of the sepulchre? And when they looked, they saw that the stone was rolled away: for it was very great.

And entering into the sepulchre, they saw a young man sitting on the right side, clothed in a long white garment; and they were affrighted. And he saith unto them, Be not affrighted: ye seek Jesus of Nazareth, which was crucified: he is risen; he is not here: behold the place where they laid him. But go your way, tell his disciples and Peter that he goeth before you into Galilee: there shall ye see him, as he said unto you.

And they went out quickly, and fled from the sepulchre; for they trembled and were amazed: neither said they any thing to any man; for they were terrified.

Mark 16: 1-8

Mark is here attempting to express in human language that which will forever surpass all human comprehension. We marvel that Mark has so skillfully and aptly recorded the terrifying experiences which happened to the three women early on Sunday morning. They come to the sepulchre intending to give careful and loving anointing to the body of Jesus, who had been so hurriedly placed in the sepulchre on Friday. On arriving at the place they find, to their amazement, that the large and heavy stone, which sealed the entrance to the cave hollowed out of solid rock, had been moved away. Entering into the sepulchre itself they at once were terrified. We need not crudely materialize the experience which met them there. Human language will always be utterly inadequate to describe supernatural experience. The heart of the matter is that in a vision and in an audition they received an understanding that a mighty act had happened — Jesus' body had been raised from the state of death, and the risen Jesus was now going ahead of them into Galilee, where they would see him. We do not wonder at the terror and trembling of the women. This new truth which they had just learned did not fit into any of the normal categories of human experience. Well might they feel terror at all of this.

It is not for us, some nineteen hundred years later, categorically to assert what God could and could not do. Nor dare we in our own pride of learning assert that the witnesses of the early church were gullible and imaginative. The unanimous witness of the four gospel traditions proclaims an empty tomb. Even though this proves a troublesome fact, not at all fitting into our own preconceptions of how God acts in his universe, we must take seriously the witness of the early Church.

However, we must carefully distinguish between the empty tomb and the resurrection appearances themselves. The empty tomb corroborates, but in no way by itself establishes, faith in the risen Christ. It is the several appearances of the risen, living Jesus that constitute the sure evidence of his resurrection, and not the empty tomb by itself. Only when the appearances are accepted does the empty tomb then fit into the whole picture.

83 RESURRECTION

Resurrection is an entirely new fact in the history of the human race. Never had it occurred before and never since. We are confronted here with that which by nature is unrepeated, unrepeatable. We are faced with an event which is unique, an event which cannot be included under any other class of events. It is upon this unique event, an act of God, that the Christian faith is founded. If this event be unhistorical and untrustworthy, then our faith has no sure foundation. The primary function of the twelve apostles in the early church was to testify to and proclaim the fact of Jesus' resurrection from the dead, and that by an action of God.

We must then refrain from seeking to interpret this resurrection by including it under other categories of human experience. Resurrection is in no way the same thing as re-animation or resuscitation. So to interpret the data goes utterly contrary to the witness and faith of the early church. The risen Jesus is no cripple, crawling about on wounded feet. The reaction of the disciples is not at all that of pity for a wounded, sick Jesus; rather he is a glorified, victorious, triumphant Jesus.

Nor can we rightly classify Jesus' resurrection under the general, philosophical category of " natural immortality of the human soul." The fact of the empty tomb, and the fact that Christianity has never had a cult of the dead body of its hero, preclude such an interpretation. Immortality implies that some hidden part of Jesus (the soul or spirit) was immortal by nature, and as such not subject to death. The spirit then, because of its own inherent nature, and not at all because of an act of God, continues its own existence in the heavenly world. But the Christian faith unequivocally proclaims that the resurrection is the action of God. Nowhere is it asserted that Jesus raised himself from death. We hear echoing and re-echoing through the early chapters of the Book of the Acts the refrain "But God raised him from the dead."

The resurrection of Jesus is an utterly new and unique event in human history, and we must humbly and reverently refrain from seeking to reduce it to any other category of human experience. Resurrection towers high above all possible known experience, like a high, forever unscalable mountain peak. We shall not be alarmed or surprised therefore to find that in the accounts describing the resurrection appearances we are faced with the supernatural.

Our earliest written evidences for the resurrection are contained in the first letter of Paul to the Christians at Corinth, where he writes:

> For I delivered unto you first of all that which I also received, how that Christ died for our sins according to the scriptures; and that he was buried, and that he rose again the third day according to the scriptures: and that he was seen of Cephas, then of the twelve. After that, he was seen of above five hundred brethren at once; of whom the greater part remain unto this present, but some are fallen asleep. After that, he was seen of James; then of all the apostles. And last of all he was seen of me also, as of one born out of due time.
>
> 1 Corinthians 15: 3-8

The original ending of Mark's account of the Gospel has been lost to us. That which he wrote in our versions ends with Verse 8 of Chapter 16. The verses which follow in our English texts were written much later and are not from the hand of Mark. When we attempt to reconstruct a probable ending to Mark's account, we presume that it contained the story of an appearance of Jesus to the disciples in Galilee, one in which Peter is especially singled out for attention. Thus in Mark 14: 28 Jesus tells his disciples, "But after that I am risen, I will go before you into *Galilee*." In Mark 16: 7 the three women are told by the angel, "But go your way, tell his disciples and Peter that he goeth before you into Galilee: *there* shall ye see him, as he said unto you." In the account given by Matthew substantially the same evidence is given. The significant passages are Matthew 26: 32; 28: 7, 10, 16. In the Lucan account however we are given no hint of any appearances in Galilee. Instead, the setting of the resurrection is Jerusalem and its environment. In the Johannine record we have stories of appearances in Jerusalem, and then in an appendix (Chapter 21) we have the story of an appearance of Jesus to the disciples in Galilee, and a story in which Peter especially figures.

We are thus confronted with a double tradition — appearances in Galilee and those in Jerusalem. John's Gospel gives us a mixture of both traditions, which fit ill together, as we shall soon see. What seems probable, in the light of the lost ending of Mark's account, is this: the first appearance of the risen Jesus to the disciples took place in Galilee, and there Peter figures prominently in one of the stories. Then the women come from Jerusalem, bringing word of the empty tomb. Sometime later Jesus commands the disciples to return to Jerusalem, where for the rest of the forty days a series of appearances occur, traces of which appear in our Lucan and Johannine Gospels. Then near by Jerusalem, perhaps at Bethany, occurs the final appearance, and its immediate sequel, the Ascension.

With this long introduction, let us now turn to what may well be our earliest tradition of the resurrection appearance of Jesus to his disciples, the story which we find in an appendix to the Johannine Gospel, in Chapter 21.

84 THE FIRST APPEARANCE

There were together Simon Peter, and Thomas called Didymus, and Nathanael of Cana in Galilee, and the sons of Zebedee, and two other of his disciples. Simon Peter saith unto them, I go a fishing. They say unto him, We also go with thee. They went forth, and entered into a ship immediately; and that night they caught nothing.

But when the morning was now come, Jesus stood on the shore: but the disciples knew not that it was Jesus. Then Jesus saith unto them, Children, have ye any meat? They answered him, No. And he said unto them, Cast the net on the right side of the ship, and ye shall find. They cast therefore, and now they were not able to draw it for the multitude of fishes. . . .

As soon then as they were come to land, they saw a fire of coals there, and fish laid thereon, and bread. . . . Jesus saith unto them, Come and dine. And none of the disciples durst ask him, Who art thou? knowing it was Jesus. Jesus then cometh, and taketh bread, and giveth them, and fish likewise.

John 21: 2-6, 9, 12-13

The twentieth chapter of the Gospel according to John ends with these words: "And many other signs truly did Jesus in the presence of his disciples, which are not written in this book: but these are written, that ye might believe that Jesus is the Christ, the Son of God; and that believing ye might have life through his name."

These words sound unmistakably like the end and conclusion of a book. Chapter twenty-one which follows is evidently an appendix, added at some later time. We can very clearly discern the editor's work in merging the story to fit in with what had been written before, i.e., verse 14, " This is now the third time that Jesus shewed himself to his disciples, after that he was risen from the dead."

We are faced here with a serious psychological difficulty. If already at Jerusalem the disciples had had two experiences of meeting the risen Jesus (the most unique, stupendous event in all human history), we wonder what in the world seven disciples are doing in Galilee fishing. It seems psychologically impossible that seven of them should leave Jerusalem for Galilee, and again take up their old vocation of fishing. However, if this story in some way represents the lost ending of Mark's account, then we can understand it better. We expect from the Marcan account that the disciples will be in Galilee, broken-hearted, listless, dejected men. What more likely than that they should go back to their old work, fishing? This story has about it the marks of a *first* meeting with the risen Jesus. It has the same quality as the Marcan account of the sacred meal near Bethsaida. Let us seek then to picture this event.

The seven disciples had been fishing all night. Did the fact that they caught nothing hint that their hearts were not in their work? Instead of giving their attention to their nets, they sat in silence, thinking back upon their life with Jesus; Peter perhaps thinking of nothing else than his denial of Jesus. As dawn comes they draw near the beach. They suddenly discern a lone figure there, which hails them. In the mists rising at early dawn from the lake, they knew not who it might be. At the command of the unknown figure they again let down their nets — they had no will of their own, but unthinkingly obeyed the command of another. Their nets, filled with squirming fish, soon brought them out of their torpor and made them wide awake.

On beaching their boat and drawing up the net to shore, they saw a fire, with fish broiling upon it, and bread. The figure bade them, "Come and dine." Suddenly their eyes were opened and they knew that it was Jesus — the Jesus whom they believed to be dead in Jerusalem. How can this thing be? They knew this was Jesus; none of them durst ask him, "Who art thou?" They knew with the certitude of sight. Then Jesus dined with them, with himself as their host. Our minds are carried back at once to the sacred meal on the hillside near Bethsaida, a sacred meal of bread and fish. One of the symbols often used by early Christians was that of a fish, with a loaf of bread upon its back. It may well be that this symbol refers to this event. Another symbol pictures a basket of fish and bread, and thus refers to the sacred meal on the hillside. But to early Christians, the former symbol would be a reminder of the first resurrection appearance, and also of the meal they had with Jesus on the beach of the Lake of Galilee. One of the Lucan stories of the resurrection also stresses Jesus' breaking of the bread. The breaking of bread, and eating, is in some very close way associated with the resurrection.

This earliest account of the resurrection in no way attempts to answer all our questions. It says nothing about the nature of Jesus' risen body. It says nothing about his coming or his going. It asserts simply and reverently the fact of his meeting with his disciples. It was not necessary that the disciples should *under-stand* how Jesus could be risen and alive. Their task was not to rationalize or understand but to testify to the fact. That it happened, not how it happened, is the important factor.

85 FORGIVENESS

So when they had dined, Jesus saith to Simon Peter, Simon, son of Jonas, lovest thou me more than these? He saith unto him, Yea, Messiah; thou knowest that I love thee. He saith unto him, Feed my lambs. He saith to him again the second time, Simon, son of Jonas, lovest thou me? He saith unto him, Yea, Messiah; thou knowest that I love thee. He saith unto him, Feed my sheep. He saith unto him the third time, Simon, son of Jonas, lovest thou me? Peter was grieved because he said unto him the third time, Lovest thou me? And he said unto him, Messiah, thou knowest all things; thou knowest that I love thee. Jesus saith unto him, Feed my sheep.

John 21: 15-17

Here is our only possible record of a special resurrection appearance of Jesus to Peter. And it is a story which has about it the very spirit of Jesus — the spirit and power of forgiving love, so characteristic of him. The threefold denial of Peter is here matched by the threefold forgiveness by Jesus. Let us picture the scene. It is early dawn on the beach at the Lake of Galilee. In silence they have just breakfasted with the risen Jesus as host; they are too amazed to speak or ask questions. It is Jesus, not they, who holds the center of attention. Their fear is gone, now replaced by awe more terrifying than their old fear. How can this be? How can this Jesus be alive, after crucifixion and burial?

Let us picture Peter, remembering his threefold denial. He does not even dare to look up into the eyes of Jesus, so shamed and broken he is by his sin. Let us envisage Peter prostrate at Jesus' feet, not daring even to touch the hem of his garments. Then let us picture Jesus stooping down to touch Peter's head, and quietly speaking to him. There is no lecture and no reproach. There is not even a hint of the past and Peter's act of denial at Jerusalem on the past Thursday night. Rather the words of Jesus deal with what Peter now is. " Simon, son of Jonas, lovest thou me more than these? " That is a question which Peter can answer from the very depth of his being,

"Messiah, thou knowest that I love thee." Peter no longer claims superiority over his fellow disciples as he had at Jerusalem — "Though all . . . yet not I." Thrice Jesus asks the question. At the third question we picture Peter looking up with agonized eyes into the eyes of the risen Jesus, "Messiah, thou knowest all things; thou knowest that I love thee." Yes, Jesus knew the depths of Peter's heart and that Peter did love him. "Feed my sheep."

In those words Jesus gave Peter free and full forgiveness, for he gave Peter a task, which he could now undertake with authority — the task of proclaiming to all men the free, full, perfect forgiveness from Jesus, forever and forever. In the Book of the Acts of the Apostles, when we again meet Peter as the spokesman of the apostolic band at Jerusalem, his great word to the people is forgiveness. Peter, who had received from the risen Jesus forgiveness, could speak with authority.

86 THE ASCENSION

Behold, I send the promise of my Father upon you: but tarry ye in the city of Jerusalem, until ye be endued with power from on high. And he led them out as far as to Bethany, and he lifted up his hands, and blessed them. And it came to pass, while he blessed them, he was parted from them, and carried up into heaven. And they worshipped him, and returned to Jerusalem with great joy: and were continually in the temple, praising and blessing God. Amen.

Luke 24: 49-53

Here again, as the last act of the earthly ministry of Jesus, we are faced with a mystery. This is the last of the resurrection appearances. No longer are they to have his sudden and mysterious meetings with them. The veil which separates the heavenly world from this earthly one falls. From now on they will know the risen Jesus only through the Spirit. The Spirit will take of the truth and life that is in Jesus, and over the years and centuries make them known to those who seek to follow Jesus. The new age of the Spirit is about to be born.

EPILOGUE

THE EARTHLY MINISTRY of Jesus is over, finished. Alone, as one sent from God, and without the help of men, Jesus has won the decisive victory over the powers of evil in the world. His work *for us* is finished. It has been offered to God, and by God accepted. Jesus has been exalted into the heavenly places, and by God seated in the place of highest honor, there to be Lord, Judge, Intercessor.

Now Jesus will send the Spirit, and through him give to us the holy, victorious life that is in himself. The victory that has been won for us must now be won *in us*, in each of us. That can be accomplished only as we humbly and meekly over the years sit at the feet of Jesus, to be taught of him of the things that belong to our salvation; and to receive from him the life that is in him. Jesus desires to be Lord of each of us. Will we let him? To surrender our lives to his Lordship is to enter, even here and now, into new life — Eternal Life.

JESUS IS LORD